SOLVE THESE F*CKING PUZZLES

Val Garrity

Publisher Mike Sanders
Editor Christopher Stolle
Designer William Thomas
Compositor Ayanna Lacey
Proofreader Amy J. Schneider
Indexer Carol Roberts

First American Edition, 2019
Published in the United States by DK Publishing
6081 E. 82nd Street, Indianapolis, Indiana 46250

Published in the United States by Dorling Kindersley Limited

ISBN 978-1-4654-8375-1
Library of Congress Catalog Number: 2019933937

DK books are available at special discounts when purchased in bulk for sales
promotions, premiums, fund-raising, or educational use. For details, contact: DK
Publishing Special Markets, 345 Hudson Street, New York, New York 10014
SpecialSales@dk.com

Printed and bound in the United States of America

All images © Dorling Kindersley Limited
For further information see: www.dkimages.com

A WORLD OF IDEAS:
SEE ALL THERE IS TO KNOW

www.dk.com

INTRODUCTION

"If you go home with somebody and they don't have books, don't fuck 'em!"
— John Waters

Truer words might never have been spoken. If you never buy another book in your life, I'm glad you bought this one. Or maybe someone gave it to you. Or maybe you're borrowing it. But whether or not there's a potential of getting laid, when someone sees this book on your coffee table or bookshelf or bathroom floor and they remark upon the wonderment of it, you've found a kindred spirit—even if in friendship if not in fornication.

"Under certain circumstances, profanity provides a relief denied even to prayer."
— Mark Twain

Words are powerful. They encourage. They appreciate. But they also infuriate, disgust, and rankle. There are no good or bad words. How you use those words is what make those words real. Some utterances are best left unsaid. You can curse your boss or a deity or even your mother—but silently in your head, from which they can't accidentally escape. There's comfort, though, in being able to express yourself in whatever way feels right to you.

"What I'm saying might be profane, but it's also profound."
— Richard Pryor

All the puzzles in this book have solutions that should make you think. You might see a lot of words you don't know or never thought you'd see in a book, let alone a puzzle book. But this free expression is how conversations begin about the state of the world, the stupidity of humans, and the stark opinions we have about anything and everything. Most of all, you should have fun trying to solve these puzzles. And you should certainly be ROTFLMAO. Enjoy!

— Val Garrity

CRYPTOGRAM? DAFUQ?

In a cryptogram, each letter of the alphabet is substituted with a different letter (substitution cipher), which are used to spell a message. To decode the message, figure out those substitutions.

___ ___ ___ ___ ___ ___ _____.
LUY VZD PUR RSD HVZ LUY OZQBD.

___'__ ___ ___ _____ __ ____
LUY'ZD PUR RSD HUPRDPRF UX LUYZ

_____. ___ ___ ___ ____
IVJJDR. LUY VZD PUR LUYZ

_____ _____.
XYHCQPM CSVCQF.

—Chuck Palahniuk

KICKING CRYPTOGRAM ASS

1. Use a pencil to jot your guesses in the blanks as you go. You might start to unveil patterns.

2. Scan through and identify single-letter words, which are likely A or I.

3. Spot the most-used ciphers, which could be substituting E, T, A, or O, especially in shorter cryptograms.

4. Punctuation can be a giveaway! For example, apostrophes are usually followed by S, T, LL, RE, and sometimes D or M.

5. Look for the repeating patterns that might indicate common letter groups, such as TH, SH, RE, CH, TR, ING, ION, and ENT.

6. Start with two-, three-, and four-letter words. Those are typically frequently used words like OF, TO, IN, IS, IT, THE, AND, FOR, and WAS.

7. Scope out double letters. They're most likely to be LL, followed in frequency by EE, SS, OO, and TT. There are other doubles (pizza, broccoli, immediately), so don't lock yourself into those four.

CRYPTOQUIZ TIME, MOTHERFUCKER:
EUPHEMISMS FOR SEXUAL INTERCOURSE

Like cryptograms, this puzzle uses a substitution cipher. All the words follow this cipher. We'll give you the first one to help you solve the rest.

AFTERNOON DELIGHT
YSLHNDMMD FHGQOWL

_____ _____
XPIUQDO POGQHJ

_____ ___
FMQDO LWH
,
_____'_ _____
FHZQG'J FYDRH

_____-_____
EQOOHNA-UMVHNA

_____ _____
VDMRVQDO XMMLJ

SHIT, NOW WHAT?

1. This is a single puzzle, so the same substitution ciphers are used in each term. Look across the whole list!

2. The puzzle title will tell you the kinds of words used. Tap into your gutter brain for inspiration.

3. Spot the most-used letters, which could be substituting E, T, A, or O, especially in shorter cryptograms.

4. Punctuation can be a giveaway! For example, apostrophes are usually followed by S, T, LL, RE, and sometimes D or M.

5. Look for the repeating letter patterns that might be common letter groups, such as TH, SH, RE, CH, TR, ING, ION, and ENT.

6. Start with two-, three-, and four-letter words. Those are typically frequently used words like OF, TO, IN, IS, IT, THE, AND, FOR, and WAS.

7. Scan for double letters. They're most likely to be LL, followed in frequency by EE, SS, OO, and TT (and on to less commonly seen doubles).

DOWNWORDS, DOGS

This is a kind of word scramble puzzle where you must find the words formed by one letter from each successive row from top to bottom. Unscramble the letters in each row to find the words in each column. This example has sex euphemisms.

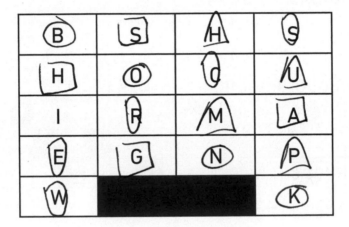

JUST THE TIPS

1. In this puzzle, two of the four words have five letters each, with only two options for the last letters. Try to work backward from them.

2. Look for the vowels. There might be common combinations that help steer.

3. Don't forget that each word has only one letter from each row. So BONE isn't one of the words, even though the letters are present.

A DROP QUOTE LESSON
BY MARC MARON

Move letters from each column down to the empty boxes below to unscramble the quote.

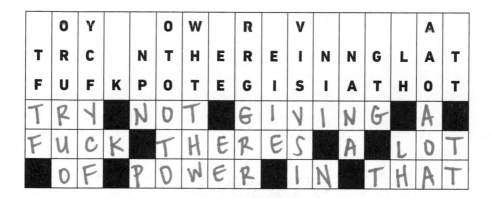

FIGURING THIS SHIT OUT

1. Look for short words and see if there are letters above to support them.

2. In this book, it's okay to search out the cusswords. They're actually supposed to be there.

3. Consider the blacked-out spaces! The puzzle reads from left to right, top to bottom. In more difficult drop quote puzzles, words might continue on the next line.

Answer: Try not giving a fuck. There's a lot of power in that. —Marc Maron

HOW THE HELL DO YOU SOLVE AN ELIMINATION QUOTE, COMRADE?

Write the word that answers all three clues. Then black out each letter in this answer in the random list of letters. What remains is an English translation of the Russian insult *"Idi nyuhai plavki!"*

1. To throw a baseball to a batter
2. The slant of a roof
3. Fever _____

_ _ _ _ _ _ _ _ _ _ _

```
I P G T O I
C S M H E T
P C L H L U
T I N P D E
R C H W I E
P A I R H T
```

WHAT THE HELL?

1. Unless otherwise indicated, there's one word that satisfies all three clues.

2. Once you have that, eliminate those letters in the puzzle. What remains is the answer.

3. There's really nothing more I can say to help with this one, bucko.

ANSWER: PITCH; Go smell underwear!

NONO-WHAT? NONOGRAMS? HUH?

Cells in the grid must be colored in according to the numbers at the top and side to reveal a picture or message. A clue of 3, 2, 3 means there are sets of 3, 2, then 3 cells shaded in with at least 1 cell between.

	5	1 1	3 5	1 1	1 1 5	5	1 1 5	1	3 1 1 1	1 1	3 5	1	3 1 1 1	1 1 1	1 3
3, 3, 3, 3															
1, 1, 1, 1, 1															
3, 1, 3, 3															
1, 1, 1, 1															
1, 3, 3, 3															
0															
3, 3, 3															
1, 1, 1, 1															
1, 1, 3, 3															
1, 1, 1, 1															
3, 1, 1															

(0 _ o)

1. This puzzle has cells in a grid that you color or leave blank depending on the numbers given at the top and side. These numbers represent "sets" and denote how many colored squares are in each row and in what groupings.

2. In this example, "3,1,3,3" means there are three sets of colored-in boxes, with a single colored box after the first colored set. You have to determine where those sets are placed and whether there's more than one space between each.

3. Go row by row, cross-checking against the columns.

4. Once you've filled in the correct boxes, they'll reveal a hidden picture.

QUOTE 'EM? NEVER HEARD OF 'EM.

The answers to the clues provide letters to help fill in the crossword. The crossword is a quote from someone famous—and famously filthy.

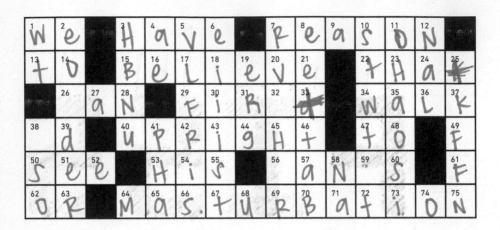

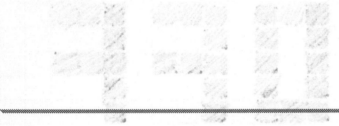

LOT OF PIECES TO THIS FUCKER

1. Each cell in the crossword has a number that can be found in the answers to the clues on the recto (elitist publisher speak for right-hand page).

2. As you fill in the crossword, you might spot words to give letters to clues to help the crossword. Synergy! Yeah!

3. Some words might go across two lines. But have patience, my friend. You'll prevail like a badass.

F U N
49 68 28
Are we having ___ yet?

H a t
3 35 13
Something to wear on your head

w a d e
34 27 39 6
Move slowly in a pool

i O N S
43 62 12 55
Atoms that gain or lose electrons

B a S k
15 57 10 37
To enjoy some sunshine

_ i N _ _ S
56 18 75 59 38 50
To prevent something from happening

F a V O R
29 24 5 14 63
A request for help

t e a R S
46 21 71 31 66
Rips or shreds

S t O R M
60 22 48 7 26
A heavy rain accompanied by thunder

L a u g H
17 4 40 44 23
A reaction to a joke

t e l e p H O N e
67 8 36 19 41 53 74 58 2
Something you use to call other people

~~F o d~~ t o t
25 11 33
Another word for a small child

F I B S
61 73 70 32
What you tell when you lie

t i M e
47 30 64 16
What a clock tells you

W a i v e R
1 65 54 20 51 42
What you sign to relinquish a claim

H e a R t
45 52 9 69 72
What beats inside your chest

CRYPTOGRAMS + MATH = DAMN IT!

Each letter in the equation is a substitution cipher for the numbers given. Find the substitutions, solve the equation, find Carmen Sandiego. Oh right, wrong game.

```
    TWIT          0  _____        5  ___E___
  + ARSE          1  _____        6  _____
  _____        2  ___T___        7  _____
    BOOB          3  _____        9  _____
                  4  _____
```

MORE TO THIS THAN SPELLING "BOOBS"
WITH YOUR CALCULATOR

1. A letter is the substitution cipher for only one number.

2. Start with the provided clues, then solve for X (heh).

3. Don't forget to carry over your numbers.

WORD CHAINS, FOOLS!

Changing only one letter at a time, each step needs to be a real word. Just because the beginning and ending words end with "-er" doesn't mean it stays that way!

MOTHER
▼
— — — — —
▼
— — — — —
▼
— — — — —
▼
— — — — —
▼
— — — — —
▼
— — — — —
▼
— — — — —
▼
— — — — —
▼
FUCKER

HUH?

1. Only one letter changes with each step.

2. Unless indicated, don't remove or add letters.

3. Each step must be a real, English word.

4. Each puzzle will have clues for every word, although they won't be in order. Here are clues for this example puzzle:

What you did in the bathtub

Another word for "smashed"

When all the water is gone: _____ dry

Someone catching rays: sun _____

Gave support to

Another word for "lollipop"

Something Pooh says: "Oh _____!"

Tanned in the sun

British term for "fired"

THE
F*CK
PUZ

KING
G
ZLES
ES

FIND THE FUCK

This puzzle might make you lose your fucking mind!
Can you find the word "FUCK" in this grid?
It appears once—and only once!

```
C K F F U C F U C U U F F U U
F F F C F C F C U F U F F C F
C F K U C U K F K C C C C F F
C K K F K C K K U U K U C F C
K C C U F C U F U F C F C F C
U F C U K U U F C F U C C K
U K U F U F C K F U F C K C F
U K K F F F U U F F U F F F K
F U U U F K U F C C F K C U U
U C U K F U U U K U C C C F U
U F C C U U K U K U C K F U C
K F U K C F F U F F U C C K U
U K C C F K U C U F C F K K F
F U K F F C K C K U F K F F C
U U C U U F C K C C K C C F K
```

SOLVE THIS FUCKING PUZZLE OR ...

If you can't figure out where to put the phrases in this crossword, then you might as well do what those phrases tell you to do.

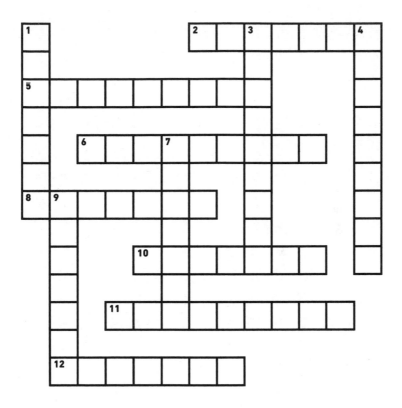

7 LETTERS
EAT SHIT

FUCK YOU

GET BENT

PISS OFF

SHOVE IT

SUCK ASS

UP YOURS

9 LETTERS
GET FUCKED

KISS MY ASS

SUCK A DICK

TAKE A HIKE

TOUGH SHIT

FIVE-FINGER SHUFFLE

Can you decode these euphemisms for masturbation?
Every phrase uses the same substitution cipher.
We've given you the first one to help you get started.
(For example: Q becomes T; H becomes U; etc.)

TUG THE SLUG
QHE QCL RZHE

_____, ___
OLDATW' QCL

_____
ECLDATW

_____ ___ _____
RBYWA QCL XUWALK

____ ___ ____
BHZZ QCL BUDA

____ ___ ____
FLYQ QCL XLYQ

____ ___ ___
GZUE QCL MUE

___ ___ _____
NYI QCL SYDDUQ

_____ ___ _____
RQDYWEZL QCL RWYAL

_____ ___ _____
SCUAL QCL SCTSALW

____ ___ _____
RZYB QCL RYZYXT

____ ___ _____
FYRC QCL FTRCUB

____ ___ _____
OYSA QCL FLYWRQYZA

DICKING AROUND

Find eight synonyms for a fella's phallus.
(Hint: One of them is "PACKAGE.")

M	P	J	M	P	S	P	S
I	E	E	O	A	A	A	A
C	U	C	N	L	C	M	H
H	A	N	K	B	K	K	S
E	M	S	A	A	E	L	O
G	R	R	O	E	I	O	G
E	■		E	D	■		N

VERY EASY WORD ARITHMETIC
Solve this puzzle using only the numbers supplied.

ASS = BAG x 2

2 ___   4 ___
3 ___   7 ___

REBUS EXCLAMATION
Give this puzzle the *middle* finger if you can't solve it.

DILLWEED & FUCKFACE

These aren't things you want to be called.

D I L L
▼

_ _ _ _
(Change one letter)
▼

_ _ _ _
(Change one letter)
▼

_ _ _ _
(Change one letter)
▼

W E E D
(Change one letter)

F U C K
▼

_ _ _ _
(Change one letter)
▼

_ _ _ _
(Change one letter)
▼

_ _ _ _
(Change one letter)
▼

F A C E
(Change one letter)

**Clues
(in no particular order)**

Metalworker's job

Boys ___ be boys

Word with oil or wishing

**Clues
(in no particular order)**

Lingerie material

Be deficient in

Shit out of ____

DOUBLE-BARRELED NONOGRAM

This puzzle is strictly for the birds.

	2	5	3 1	5 2 2	2 4 2 6	1 4 2 6	5 8	5 8	1 1 2 2 6	2 4 2 6	5 2 2	3 1	5	2
6														
2, 2, 2														
1, 2, 1														
8														
1, 5, 2, 1														
1, 3, 3, 1														
1, 6, 1														
3, 2, 3														
4, 2, 4														
10														
6														
2														
2														
4														
2, 2														
2, 2														
2, 2														
2, 2														
3, 3														
3, 3														

MARILYN MANSON

This hard rocker has some advice about communication.

```
____ __ ___ _____'_ _____
CEFW ET WMY NEJRI'F UJELRYCF

_____ __ _____ __ _____ ____
HESRI LY BAEZIYI ZT UYEURY DSFW

____ ____ ____ _____ _____.
FBZI NMBW WMYX TSHPZKQ CYBKW.
```

BARNYARD PICTOGRAM

Care for a cuppa while you solve this puzzle?

OBSCENE TELEPHONE

Marty works at a cell phone company and is in charge of assigning phone numbers to new customers. One of his favorite pranks is to hide insulting words or phrases in the numbers he hands out to particularly annoying customers. See if you can find the hidden insults in each of the following nine telephone numbers.
(Use the provided keypad as a reference.)

1	**2** ABC	**3** DEF
4 GHI	**5** JKL	**6** MNO
7 PQRS	**8** TUV	**9** WXYZ
*	**0**	#

879-6877

438-2368

277-4653

227-8273

342-5923

382-5948

744-8224

386-2277

724-6825

URGENT PICTOGRAM

Get to the nitty-gritty with this puzzle.

GILLIAN ANDERSON

This actress is all about being abnormal.

```
____ _ _____ __ _____,
DAUB O FAOBC EY BETNLQJK,
_ _____ __ _____-___ _____
O FAOBC EY NUIOEJTOFK-LBI NUIOEJTOFK
_____ ___ _____ ___ __ __.
WJLTUW FAU YGJC EGF EY NU.
```

NONOGRAM ADVICE

If you're going to go somewhere, then go ...

	5 3 3 1	1 1 3 1 1 1	1 1 3 1 3	0	5 5 5	1 1 1 1 1 1	5 5 5 1	0	5 5 5	1 1 1 1	1 1 5 5	0	5 5 5	1 1 2 1	2 2 3 1 1 1
3, 1, 1, 3, 1, 1															
1, 1, 1, 1, 1, 1															
3, 1, 1, 1, 2															
1, 1, 1, 1, 1, 1															
1, 3, 3, 1, 1															
0															
1, 1, 3, 1, 1, 3															
1, 1, 1, 1, 1, 1, 1, 1															
3, 1, 1, 1, 1, 3															
1, 1, 1, 1, 1, 2															
1, 3, 3, 1, 1															
0															
3, 3, 1, 3															
1, 1, 1, 1															
3, 2, 1, 3															
1, 1, 1, 1															
3, 3, 3, 1															

FOODIE PICTOGRAM
Hungry to solve this puzzle?

JEN FAULKNER
Hemingway and Melville understand the struggle.

```
                          "
____ _____ ___ "_____ ___
VFTB XTJXIT DSQ "GFTWT SWT

_____ ____ __ ___ ___," _ ___:
JGFTW AHDF HB GFT DTS," H DSQ:
 "____ ___, ___ ___ __ ___."
 "AKPL QJK, DFT VSD YQ DTS."
```

PROFANITY PROFICIENCY

All these terms are archaic insults that are no longer in common English usage. Test your ability to see how many you can define correctly!

BEARD-SPLITTER

a. A person who regularly visits prostitutes

b. Someone who constantly lies

c. A silly-looking person with no style

d. Someone who can never make up their mind

ABYDOCOMIST

a. A stupid, useless person

b. One who lies often and is proud of it

c. A fraud doctor

d. Someone who has sex with their own relatives

ROIDERBANKS

a. A horse thief

b. A fat-bottomed person

c. One who spends beyond their means

d. Someone constantly filled with rage

SCOBBERLOTCHER

a. An idle, lazy person

b. A thief

c. Someone with perpetually dirty feet

d. A person who speaks nonsensically

SMELLFUNGUS

a. Someone with horrible body odor

b. A thieving priest

c. A nosy, prying person

d. A fault-finding buzzkill

BOBOLYNE

a. An ample-chested female

b. A merchant who charges far too much

c. A stupid fool

d. A quack doctor

RAKEFIRE

a. A coward who stirs trouble and then runs

b. A guest who overstays their welcome

c. An inveterate womanizer

d. Someone who spreads lies about others

SNOUTBAND

a. A know-it-all who constantly interrupts other people

b. Someone with an unusually large, aquiline nose

c. Someone fond of performing cunnilingus

d. A son of a whore

RANTALLION

a. A rambunctious child

b. An excessively cheap person

c. A guy with a small dick

d. Someone who's constantly yelling

SKELPIE-LIMMER

a. One who fornicates with animals

b. A rambunctious, naughty young girl

c. A fat person in ill-fitting clothing

d. Someone who smells like rotting fish

Step proudly into that spotlight!

K I N G O F T H E W O R L D
33 60 9 61 114 43 29 48 35 13 97 59 82 92

"I'm the _____" (Titanic boast)

N e w Y o r k C i t y
2 54 113 39 42 38 105 74 10 50 17

The Big Apple

___ ___ ___ ___ ___ ___ ___ ___ ___ ___ ___ ___ ___ ___
116 75 41 46 72 107 53 80 83 6 36 26 15 79 4

Mona Lisa painter

___ ___ ___ ___ ___ ___ ___ ___ ___ ___
96 49 64 111 19 90 20 85 5 28 65

Renaissance author of The Prince

___ ___ ___ ___ ___ ___ ___ ___ ___
70 95 101 106 16 104 57 45 55

Emergency conveyance

___ ___ ___ ___ ___ ___ ___ ___ ___
76 27 81 11 77 18 68 32 91

Illicit pool of money

___ ___ ___ ___ ___ ___ ___
102 108 24 99 109 21 71

Sexy stocking style

T H e t R U T H
110 62 100 63 115 51 47 22

"You can't handle _____!" (famous Jack Nicholson line)

B I T E S T H E D U S T
89 31 12 14 94 3 87 93 117 103 34 86

"Another One _____" (Queen song)

___ ___ ___ ___ ___
37 8 56 7 23

Get bent!

___ ___ ___ ___ ___ ___ ___
84 1 25 67 30 112 66

Sausage seller

___ ___ ___ ___ ___ ___ ___ ___ ___
98 88 73 78 69 58 52 44 40

Run-down apartments

WHO GIVES A FUCK?

You will if you want to solve this puzzle! Give a "fuck"
to each of these unfinished terms by adding the letters
F, **U**, **C**, and **K** in any order to reveal each answer below.

_R_IT_A_E
Traditional holiday snack

HOC __LL
Jam-packed

__LLBA__
Football position

JA___R_IT
Southeast Asian staple

_N_RO__
Remove from the priesthood

H___ _INN
Twain character, for short

__F_LIN_
Fancy fastener

DA_FY D___
Bugs Bunny's foil

_IRE TR___
Red emergency vehicle

WHO GIVES A SHIT?

Give a "shit" to each of these unfinished terms by adding the letters **S**, **H**, **I**, and **T** *in that order* to reveal each answer. For example, ASU becomes **SHI**AT**S**U.

F   _ _ _ _ _

OPLF   _ _ _ _ _ _ _

PMEN   _ _ _ _ _ _ _

MAOCS   _ _ _ _ _ _ _ _

CNZEL   _ _ _ _ _ _ _ _

GEUNDE   _ _ _ _ _ _ _ _ _

YPILIC   _ _ _ _ _ _ _ _ _

FLALGH   _ _ _ _ _ _ _ _ _

PYCOLOGS   _ _ _ _ _ _ _ _ _ _ _

OPSTICAED   _ _ _ _ _ _ _ _ _ _ _ _

MITCH HEDBERG

Just chalk this one up to function over flavor.

```
____ ___ _____ _____
BCTJ PWJ GKEVBPBNVTP MEBWIEVP
___ _____.  ___ _____ ___
WUT QCTYWLKT.  WKK MEBWIEVP WUT
_____-__'_ ____ ____
QCTYWLKT—EB'P FXPB BCWB
____ _____ _____.
BCTJ BWPBT PCEBBJ.
```

RUST COHLE

This *True Detective* character speaks of the Golden Rule.

```
__ ___ ____ _____ _____ _
VS URQ ZGDK URVGW LQQXVGW E
_____ _____ __ ___ _____
XQTIZG PQHQGU VI URQ QAXQHUEUVZG
__ _____ _____, ____' _____,
ZS PVMVGQ TQNETP, URQG, OTZURQT,
____ _____ __ _ _____ __ ____.
UREU XQTIZG VI E XVQHQ ZS IRVU.
```

EASY WORD ARITHMETIC

Solve these puzzles using only the numbers supplied.

```
        ANUS        0  T        6  ___
  +      ASS         4  ___      7  ___
  _____
        BUTT        5  ___      8  ___
```

```
        SHIT        0  ___      4  ___      8  ___
  +      PISS         1  T        5  ___
  _____
       TUSHY        3  S        6  ___
```

```
      MIDDLE        0  ___      4  ___      8  ___
  + FINGER          1  ___      5  ___      9  ___
  _____
      OFFERED       2  E        6  ___
                    3  ___      7  D
```

MEDIUM WORD ARITHMETIC

Solve these puzzles using only the numbers supplied.

```
    SHIT       0 _1_    3 ___    6 ___
+   BITCH      1 ___    4 ___    7 ___
+ ASSHAT       2 ___    5 _M_    8 ___
─────────
   DAMMIT
```

```
   SWEAR       0 ___    4 ___    8 ___
+  CURSE       1 ___    5 _E_    9 ___
─────────      2 _R_    6 ___
  WICKED       3 ___    7 ___
```

```
  ASSHAT       1 ___    4 ___    7 _y_
- SHITTY       2 ___    5 ___    8 ___
─────────      3 _T_    6 ___
   BITCH
```

WORDOKU

USE THESE LETTERS: **K E N W R A**

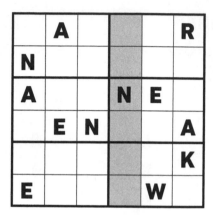

WORDOKU

USE THESE LETTERS: **I U D N S G**

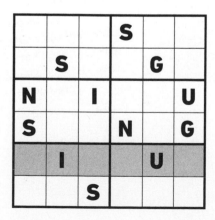

MEDIUM WORD ARITHMETIC

Solve these puzzles using all the numbers from 0 to 9 so both equations are simultaneously true.

$$\begin{array}{r} \text{BAG} \\ \times \quad \text{OF} \\ \hline \text{DICKS} \end{array} \qquad \begin{array}{r} \text{BACK} \\ + \quad \text{OFF} \\ \hline 4466 \end{array}$$

0 ____   4 ____   8 ____

1 ____   5 ____   9 _f_

2 _G_   6 ____

3 ____   7 ____

Handy Diagram

"duck"

"fuck"

We process swear words in an entirely different and deeper part of the brain (the limbic system and basal ganglia) than all other language, which is usually handled by the cerebral cortex.

BALLS DEEP

Don't be a dick—find the synonyms for testicles.

```
S G O N A D S G O S C J V
I B N A Q D J R J C C H S
W O Y R N L H A B W S E I
I Q S D S U I P V I L O C
K P K S E L T E L G C N O
T C C V U L S N N B S I
A T O B R O V A R I E S N
E S L V E F J S B I A Q P
M V L H M O T G L C N I U
H J O J B O U B K H B J R
L O B P N L U C B H A K S
C Y W E J J C Y Y Y G V E
F X S G I B L E T S G F J
```

Balls   Grapes

Beanbag   Huevos

Bojangles   Jublies

Bollocks   Meat Kiwis

Brovaries   Nards

Coin Purse   Nuts

Giblets   Sack

Gonads   Stones

SPANISH INSULTS

Can you decode these Spanish insults? We've translated them into English and encrypted them using the same substitution cipher. (Hints: T = S and B = H.)

‾ ‾‾‾‾ ‾‾‾ ‾‾‾ ‾‾‾‾‾‾ ‾‾ ‾ ‾‾‾‾!
J BQML HQG OLK NGVYLP DH C NJTB!

‾ ‾‾‾‾ ‾‾ ‾‾‾ ‾‾‾‾!
J TBJK JU KBL RJXY!

‾ ‾‾‾‾ ‾‾ ‾‾‾ ‾‾‾‾‾ ‾‾‾‾
J TBJK JU KBL ZBQIL KBCK
‾‾‾‾ ‾‾‾‾‾‾ ‾‾ ‾‾‾!
OCFL DJIKB KQ HQG!

‾‾‾ ‾‾‾‾‾‾‾'‾ ‾‾‾‾‾!
KBL MCIIQK'T MGTTH!

LOUIS CK

Cross out every **H, N, R, U,** and **Y** in this list of letters and what remains will be an insult popularized by Louis CK.

NEYANTRU

HUNANYRH

YRBUHIRGY

UBRNAYUG

RYONUFHR

YDUICHKRS

ASSHOLE & BULLSHIT

These *do* sort of go together.

A S S		B U L L
▼		▼
_ _ _ _		_ _ _ _
(Add one letter)		*(Change one letter)*
▼		▼
_ _ _ _		_ _ _ _
(Change one letter)		*(Change one letter)*
▼		▼
_ _ _ _		_ _ _ _
(Change one letter)		*(Change one letter)*
▼		▼
_ _ _ _		_ _ _ _
(Anagram)		*(Anagram)*
▼		▼
H O L E		S H I T
(Change one letter)		*(Change one letter)*

Clues **(in no particular order)**	**Clues** **(in no particular order)**
At a ____ for words	Slang for vagina
Girl, in Scotland	Window feature
Shoe part	Bird's beak
Misplace	River deposit

GEN. JAMES "MAD DOG" MATTIS

Solve this puzzle—and that's an order!

_ ____ __ _____. _ ____',
P JVUS PD FSEJS. P CPCD'W

_____ _____. ___ ____, P'U _____
QKPDB EKWPZZSKG. QTW P'U FZSECPDB

____ ___, ____ _____ __ __ ____:
NPWR GVT, NPWR WSEKX PD UG SGSX:

__ ___ ____ ____ __',
PI GVT ITJY NPWR US,

_'__ ____ ___ ___.
P'ZZ YPZZ GVT EZZ.

OZZY FUCKING OSBOURNE

This is a pretty clear statement.

_'_ ___ _____ __ ___ ____.
U'X KEC DUSBUKV ID QEV FWUC.

_'_ _ ____ ____.
U'X O JESB FCOJ.

BUTTHOLE & CRAPHOLE

These might seem less vulgar, but they can still sting.

B U T T
▼
_ _ _ _
(Change one letter)
▼
_ _ _ _
(Change one letter)
▼
_ _ _ _
(Change one letter)
▼
_ _ _ _
(Change one letter)
▼
H E A D
(Change one letter)

**Clues
(in no particular order)**

Word with dead or wave

____ off (choke the chicken)

Woman's chest

Cream of the crop

C R A P
▼
_ _ _ _
(Anagram)
▼
_ _ _ _
(Change one letter)
▼
_ _ _ _
(Change one letter)
▼
_ _ _ _
(Change one letter)
▼
H O L E
(Change one letter)

**Clues
(in no particular order)**

____ and hearty

Tortoise rival

Bottom-feeding fish

Give a fuck

COMPOUND CUSSIN'

These terms have much more impact than if these compound words were split up. Can you find them all?

H K T Y K U L Y X D N A T X L
Y E I K C C O C X M O K D S M
K B H Z J A O M A U T B I Y V
O V S V T S Q L K D K X P C O
M F N L K S X L J D C E S P L
C Z E L E B W J R A U T H K W
V O K X V A E A Y E F W I Z S
G B C N X G Z S Q W I D T Y Q
A U I K V I F I E G E J Z B G
I T H M W P E C K E R H E A D
W F C T I A W N W U J L S Q A
Q K I E C A F K C U F Z E W I
I H P J A Y C F U J H Q I K S
S B Y K E I G H L U B C C L R
Z Z F G D B N Z J E L I L Q M

Assbag   Fuckface
Chickenshit   Fuckton
Cockwaffle   Peckerhead
Dickweed   Shitwizard
Dipshit

CONCEALED COCKS

Dr. Ron Everhardt is a renowned Dark Ages historian and a bit of a prankster. He surreptitiously hid 16 synonyms for "cock" in the first two paragraphs of his latest dissertation. Can you find them all? (We've bolded the first one to help you out.)

In the year 672, a band of Nor**DIC K**nights on their way to reach Odessa were encamped at the snowy base of Mount Ezekiel. Basalt cliffs 1,000 feet high hemmed them in on three sides. Altofor, gang leader of this paltry band, looked like any other Norseman: hooded simply in stiff, drab leather. Ordinarily, he would don green headgear and a triumphal lustrous coat of armor—but not today. A passing shepherd would think no better of it to see such a traveler in these parts and such anonymity would prove advantageous.

As day turned to night and Altofor stared deeply into the glum embers of his fading fire, he smiled to himself as he imagined how angry the Odessans—who put zero thought into fortifying themselves from a southern attack—would be tomorrow morning and how much he'd enjoy sticking his blade through the chest of King John's only living son, leaving his naked, frozen corpse in the frozen slush afterward as a reminder to all that the pen is still not mightier than the sword.

HEATHER CHANDLER

This is just one of many great lines from *Heathers*.

‾‾‾‾ ‾‾ ‾‾‾‾‾‾ ‾‾‾‾ ‾ ‾‾‾‾‾‾‾‾‾.
VNJT YW IWRHKB DOHG X JGXORCXD.

DOROTHY PARKER

Either way, something's going on.

‾‾‾‾ ‾‾‾ ‾ ‾‾‾ ‾‾‾ ‾‾‾‾‾‾‾ ‾‾‾‾‾
XCBB JRT R MPL XAA EZIHRWU SZLO—
‾‾ ‾‾‾‾ ‾‾‾‾‾.
AF QRIC QCFLP.

WORDOKU

USE THESE LETTERS: **G O H C A E D B U**

			C		H	B		
	U			E			A	H
	O			U		E		
		H			G		E	
		C	D		U	A		
		D		O			H	
		O		B				G
B	G		E					H
			E	H		O		

A popular translation program released in 2002 mistakenly rendered the simplified Chinese character meaning "dry" or "dried" as "fuck," resulting in thousands of machine-translated Chinese restaurant menus containing items such as "fuck the fruit" (dried fruit) or "fuck the cuttlefish" (dried cuttlefish).

DICKHEAD & HOLY SHIT
Welcome to the Church of Vulgarity.

D I C K
▼

_ _ _ _
(Change one letter)
▼

_ _ _ _
(Change one letter)
▼

_ _ _ _
(Change one letter)
▼

_ _ _ _
(Anagram)
▼

H E A D
(Change one letter)

H O L Y
▼

 _ _ _
(Change one letter)
▼

_ _ _ _
(Change one letter)
▼

_ _ _ _
(Change one letter)
▼

_ _ _ _
(Anagram)
▼

S H I T
(Change one letter)

**Clues
(in no particular order)**

Word with wolf or straits

Roll the _____

Got between the covers, say

Truth or _____

**Clues
(in no particular order)**

Party thrower

Word with garden or panty

Word with money or body

Word with pie or ass

BASIC BITCH & FUCK SHIT

Don't be someone stupid who doesn't know anything.

B A S I C

_ _ _ _ _
(Change one letter)

_ _ _ _
(Remove one letter)

_ _ _ _
(Change one letter)

_ _ _ _
(Change one letter)

_ _ _ _ _
(Add one letter)

B I T C H

F U C K

_ _ _ _
(Change one letter)

_ _ _ _
(Change one letter)

_ _ _ _
(Change one letter)

_ _ _ _
(Change one letter)

_ _ _ _
(Anagram)

S H I T

Clues
(in no particular order)

Big party

Cookie quantity

Word with bubble or bomb

On a first-name ____

Stereo knob

Clues
(in no particular order)

Rear end

Do a street performance

"___ the fuck up!"

Slang for a woman's pubic hair

Pass the ____

OH NO! BETTE MIDLER!
Not sure these words fit with a proper tune.

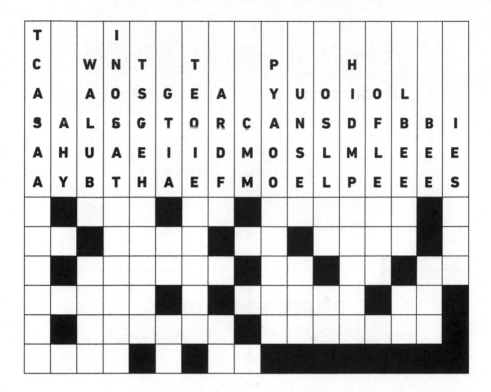

W.C. FIELDS
He had a thirst for something else anyhow.

```
_ ___,_ _____ _____. ____ ____ __ __.
U GRT'V GOUTY HMVBO. PUKC PJEY UT UV.
```

TINA FEY

This funny lady has a zinger
about the potential pitfalls of technology.

```
_____ __ ____ ____ _____.
VYLDLRYLV AR MNRD EAZX GPZXNV.
____ __'_ ____ ____', __ _____ _____,
CYXJ AD'R TLJX CXEE, AD ELLZR QWXPD,
___ ____ __'_ _____', ___ ____
PJT CYXJ AD'R LKXWTLJX, OLN ELLZ
____ _ _____ _____.
EAZX P HWPUO PRRYLEX.
```

ROBIN WILLIAMS

They *just* have to sit right *on* you.

```
_ _____ ____ _____ _____
X RAULBN RYFK DYFXNT KYXUP
_____ ___ ___: "__ ____ _____
FCAOK FEE LFM: "AY YBNB DASBT
_____ _____."
FUAKYBN FTTYAEB."
```

PRICK & LOSER
Solve this to become a prickless winner. Wait. What?

P R I C K

_ _ _ _
(Change one letter)

_ _ _ _
(Remove one letter)

_ _ _ _
(Change one letter)

_ _ _ _
(Change one letter)

_ _ _ _
(Change one letter)

L O S E R
(Add one letter)

Clues
(in no particular order)

Romantic flower

Haggler's concern

Win, ____, or draw

California roll ingredient

____ and shine

MILES DAVIS

If you've heard this badass cat play his trumpet,
you know he speaks the truth.

```
 _ _ _ _ _ _ _   _ _ _   _ _ _ _ .   _ _ _   _ _ _ _   _ _
 XFAKPQA  NXF  MDXA .   WRS   FPWS   VB

 _ _ _ _   _ _ _ _ _ _   _ _ _ _ _ _ .   _ _ _   _ _ _ _ _ _ _
 PFDA  WESFWA  MSINSFW .   WRS   XWWVWYQS

 _ _   _ _ _   _ _ _ _ _ _ _ _ _ _ _   _ _ _   _ _ _ _ _   _ _
 PU  WRS  GPWRSIUYNTSI  ERP  MDXAB  VW

 _ _   _ _ _ _ _ _   _ _ _ _ _ _ _ .
 VB  SVORWA  MSINSFW .
```

ANONYMOUS

This should be everyone's mantra.

```
            ,
 _ _   _ _ _   _ _ _ ' _   _ _ _   _ _   _ _ _   _ _   _ _ _
 CO  HGX  BGY'L  RCZ  CY  AZB  ML  GYZ
                                     "
 _ _   _ _ _   _ _ _ _ _ _ _   _ _ _   _ _ _ _ _   " _ _ _ _   _ _ _
 CY  LSZ  JGIYCYP  MYB  LSCYF  "KSML  LSZ
                                            ,"
 _ _ _ _   _ _   _ _ _ _ _   _ _ _ _   _ _   _ _ _ _ , "
 OXWF  MJ  C  BGCYP  KCLS  JH  RCOZ , "
    ,
 _ _ _ ' _ _   _ _ _ _ _   _ _ _ _ _ _ _ _ _ _   _ _ _ _ _ .
 HGX'IZ  BGCYP  VGJZLSCYP  KIGYP .
```

CLOSE TO THE CHEST

Don't be a tit—just find these synonyms for boobies.

```
D Y H B S R E K N O H D C
S P B C S T U N O C O C H
T G O X H Q X M E A O Q A
O F S K A E P N I W T Z C
L W O I S S S R M E V H
M I M R A P T T A G R U A
N X S S T S T M I M S S S
K C A R A C M N E C B W J
N A X E T A R L Z O L I W
O C R K R W O E O V S E L
R B N I X N Q B R H G E S
D Z E Q S S G A B N U F Y
M S A B M O O Z A B J W O
```

Bazoombas	Honkers
Boobs	Hooters
Bosoms	Jugs
Breasts	Mammaries
Cha-Chas	Melons
Chesticles	Rack
Coconuts	Tatas
Funbags	Twin Peaks

ANONYMOUS
We're on a rock in space. Get over yourself!

__ ___ ____ _____ _____ ___
DY THX NMNO JAUOA APDWCDWZ AHH

_____ __ _____, ____ ____
PDZPGT HY THXOJNGY, YDWS THXO

_____ _____ __ _____ ____
KXOONWA QHJDADHW HW ZHHZGN LUQJ

___ ____ ___ ____ ___.
UWS EHHL APN YXKC HXA.

DAN SAVAGE
That's quite a papal smear.

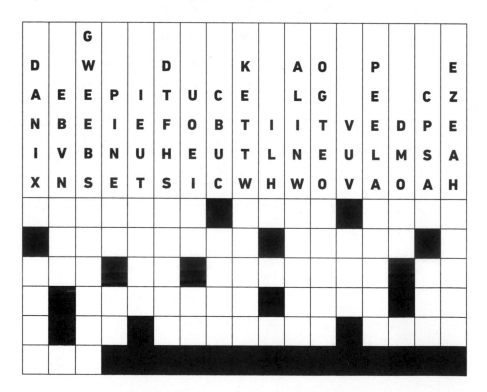

HERE, KITTY KITTY

Slip your way into this puzzle by finding the euphemisms for female genitalia.

```
V Q T N R R M P Q K U I U
L O I D H U E W L E E B T
I O L Q F E J I G K Y D A
V L S F U L N N P O G Y P
B G Y I B I I F L B N T E
V I N N P M M Z H E W H N
A K N V H S Y C J A K A I
J L A A N L T H T V K H S
A I F G Y A G Q C E I O F
Y S E I H C F R V R T O L
J M I N N I E L Y R T H Y
A S U A F T J D O S Y W T
Y F Q C O R H X I W S D R
S X E O Z E C R G R E U A
F S C L O V E B O X M R P
```

Beaver	Love Box	Silk Igloo
Cooter	Minge	Slit
Fanny	Minnie	Twat
Flower	Muff	Vagina
Fun Hatch	Penis Fly Trap	Vajayjay
Hoohah	Pussy	Vertical Smile
Kitty	Quim	

TURKISH INSULT

Write the word that answers all three clues. Then black out each letter in this answer in the random list of letters on the next page. What remains is an English translation of the Turkish insult *Ağzına sıçarım!*

1. Male member
2. Word with care or deal
3. UPS delivery

_ _ _ _ _ _

-POSTED-
All vulgarity must now be spoken before entering temple.

The English word "profanity" comes from the Latin word, profanus, which combines pro (before) and fanus (temple) to denote something that is wicked or impious; literally, something only to be done before entering a holy place.

PIAKLCL

KSEHCIC

TPGIKNP

YKOAUAR

MOCUTAH

SAY AGAIN?

You'll be a twit if you can't find all these words that sound naughty but aren't.

```
D  B  I  O  A  N  I  G  N  A  B  K  C
N  A  D  I  G  Y  C  T  W  E  L  Q  A
U  U  T  I  T  M  O  U  S  E  O  C  Z
B  R  V  C  N  C  L  U  B  D  W  O  L
R  A  N  E  L  G  N  O  D  N  H  C  A
E  L  E  P  S  Z  H  F  T  U  O  C  B
M  T  M  I  V  U  I  Y  N  C  L  Y  I
M  N  A  A  A  R  N  H  H  E  E  X  L
U  A  E  N  K  S  Y  A  P  F  P  T  B
C  T  S  I  T  S  A  E  R  B  A  A  K
Y  X  N  S  V  E  N  U  V  U  L  A  L
Q  E  Q  T  G  A  K  L  U  A  C  F  Q
W  S  V  N  L  J  J  E  D  C  F  X  X
```

Abreast	Cummerbund	Pianist
Angina	Dinghy	Seamen
Aural	Dongle	Sextant
Balzac	Fecund	Titmouse
Blowhole	Firkin	Uranus
Caulk	Nepal	Uvula
Coccyx	Penal	

STACEYANN CHIN

This spoken-word poet echoes sentiments
by Lucille Clifton but punches them up some more.

```
 _,  _  _____.  ____ _____ _ _____ ____.
E'W  X  HCWXQ.  PDXP WYXQK E UGYXB DXGM.
 ___ ____ ____ _ _____
 XQM WYQM ZEBY X WCPDYGSJLBYG—
 ___ ____ ___ ____ __ _____ _____
 XZZ KYTI XQM SJZZ CS DYXGP UGYXBEQVZI
      _____ _____.
      UYXJPESJZ KLXGK.
```

DAVID BOWIE

He's a starman who transcended this earthly plane.

```
 _ ____ ____ ____ __ _ _____.
 U JHFY GHPK SQMK OT O IQLOM.
 _ _____:  "____ ____. _ ____
 U YIEQNIY:  "JQAB YIOY. U COMY
      __ __ _ _____."
      YE XH O TQSHPIQLOM."
```

My Name Is
Roger
Fuckebythenavele

Court records from the year 1310 show that an Englishman with the unusual name of "Roger Fuckebythenavele" was banished from Chester County for unspecified reasons.

GERMAN INSULT

Write the word that answers all three clues. Then black out each letter in this answer in the random list of letters on the next page. What remains is an English translation of the German insult
Ihre Mutter säugt Schweine!

1. Word with boat or split
2. Good source of potassium
3. _____ hammock (speedo)

_ _ _ _ _ _

The oldest "rude" English word that still retains its original meaning is "fart," which dates back all the way to 1250.

BYNOAUBR
AMBOTNHA
ENRBSAUN
ACBKLNES
NPAINGSB

QUEEN'S ENGLISH

Don't be a manky minger, you daft cow.
Find these insults from the British vernacular.

```
Y X R K P N Q C R T J G S
N M R T S F V F E N Q K R
R E K N O L P F G U F N N
B B C E N S C A D C D O U
J L O Q D W S N O I Y B M
C O F B I N T E C R E H P
C O F E C K E X R O M E T
E M O J Q V J L O T I A Y
L I D Q M T A V L T L D Q
V N O W C W E H E E B D R
Q G S G A A D M C R B T K
Z A L I C T P I L L O C K
L C C A K B L I G H T E R
```

Bellend	Chav	Pillock
Berk	Codger	Plonker
Bint	Cunt	Rotter
Blighter	Feck	Sod Off
Blimey	Knobhead	Tosser
Blooming	Naff	Twat
Cack	Numpty	

FULL OF SHIT

We dumped a pile of letters on this page.
Can you find all the words related to a shitty situation?

```
C  G  T  M  X  T  A  P  E  S  H  I  T
E  S  I  A  S  H  I  T  S  H  O  W  T
G  C  H  H  L  F  S  H  J  T  F  I  L
P  G  S  I  I  E  I  Y  S  A  U  A  H
U  I  E  N  T  T  B  Z  H  L  L  O  T
R  V  S  P  T  B  U  E  I  K  L  Q  W
S  E  R  Y  L  W  A  R  T  Y  O  U  Q
H  A  O  B  E  T  X  G  S  C  F  M  B
I  S  H  N  S  L  S  H  T  Z  S  Y  J
T  H  F  H  B  I  N  O  S  H  I  T
F  I  I  J  I  T  G  A  R  T  I  H  S
I  T  B  O  T  T  B  W  M  U  T  E  Z
T  I  H  S  R  I  T  S  U  T  S  C  C
```

Apeshit	No shit
Bullshit	Shit bag
Eat shit	Shit fit
Full of shit	Shitrag
Give a shit	Shitshow
Holy shit	Shitstorm
Horseshit	Shitty
Little shit	Stir shit

BIBLICAL REBUS

Say a little prayer that you can figure this one out.

E

J.D. SALINGER

In *The Catcher in the Rye*, Holden Caulfield kept looking
for a peaceful place but learned a hard lesson.

____ ___'__ ___ _____,
TWDQ XZL'SD QZO RZZAKQJ,

_____'__ _____ __ ___ _____
MZYDPZUX'RR MQDCA LE CQU TSKOD

"____ ___" _____ _____ ____ ____.
"NLFA XZL" SKJWO LQUDS XZLS QZMD.

JOHN GREEN

In *Looking for Alaska*, The Colonel does some quick math to assess Pudge's current physical state.

G͟ C͟H͟Q͟Z͟ E͟G͟E͟ Q͟J͟P͟S͟ D͟N͟V͟D͟H͟V͟N͟Z͟G͟J͟F͟Q͟
,
N͟F͟E͟ G͟'͟A͟S͟ U͟S͟S͟F͟ N͟U͟V͟S͟ Z͟J͟ E͟S͟Z͟S͟W͟P͟G͟F͟S͟
,
Z͟Y͟N͟Z͟ K͟J͟H͟'͟W͟S͟ L͟H͟V͟V͟ J͟L͟ Q͟Y͟G͟Z͟.

CRANIAL PICTOGRAM

You'll solve this puzzle if you don't fit this description.

HARD WORD ARITHMETIC

Solve this puzzle using only the numbers supplied.

```
              FACE
          _____
FUCK ) ASSHOLE
       – HKHF
       _____
         KKLFO
       – KUSAA
       _____
         KACSL
       – KHHLC
       _____
         KFHFE
       – KFHFE
       _____
             U
```

Hint: *This notation tells you that FUCK x F = HKHF;*
FUCK x A = KUSAA; FUCK x C = KHHLC; and FUCK x E = KFHFE.

0 ___		**4** ___		**8** ___	
1 ___		**5** ___		**9** ___	
2 ___		**6** *E*			
3 ___		**7** ___			

HARD WORD ARITHMETIC

Solve this puzzle using only the numbers supplied.

$$
\require{enclose}
\begin{array}{r}
\phantom{\text{EAT}\,}\text{MY} \\
\text{EAT}\,\enclose{longdiv}{\text{FARTS}} \\
-\,\text{FTSS} \\
\hline
\text{RRTS} \\
-\,\text{RRTS} \\
\hline
\text{S}
\end{array}
$$

Hint: *This notation tells you that EAT x M = FTSS and EAT x Y = RRTS.*

0 ___	3 ___	6 ___
1 ___	4 ___	7 A
2 ___	5 ___	

Giving someone the middle finger dates back all the way to antiquity! It was considered an insulting gesture by the Greeks at least as far back as the 5th century B.C.

WORDOKU

USE THESE LETTERS: **C A M I G B H T E**

		C	T				G	A
T						I		B
			A	B				
		E				G		C
H				C				E
G		B				H		
			M	A				
B		M						G
C	I			T	E			

In the 16th century, common kestrels (a type of falcon) were called windfuckers.

FOUR-LETTER WORDS

Go beyond "fuck" and "shit" to find
some other popular four-letter terms.

```
B A M L Z I S X M N O B G
Y Y Z U R M Q R G J H K I
V Y C T F S S G U J P U S
J R R W U F D I D D I F G
T N B R A P I L J C M G B
W N X R A V E U H A P T N
S J T G F S K J D S T T W
P K C A R I S N V I C D T
A M J A S G C B O O B A Y
R Q X L A F L I M B M Y G
C K I S N A D S S T I E R
U T H W U P X F T N U C O
Y W Z X S Q P Y B P Q I S
```

Anus	Jism	Pimp
Arse	Jugs	Putz
Boob	Knob	Quim
Crap	Milf	Rack
Cunt	Muff	Scag
Fart	Nads	Slit
Gash	Orgy	

HARUKI MURAKAMI

This Japanese writer cuts to the chase—and cuts deep.

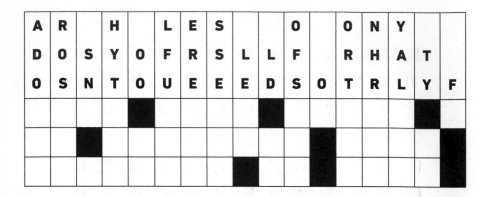

A	R		H		L	E	S		O		O	N	Y			
D	O	S	Y	O	F	R	S	L	L	F		R	H	A	T	
O	S	N	T	O	U	E	E	E	D	S	O	T	R	L	Y	F

STEPHEN KING

That's an accurate acronym.

‾‾‾‾ ‾‾‾‾‾‾ ‾‾‾
NCQU MZQIYM NPU

‾‾‾‾ ‾‾‾‾‾‾‾‾‾‾ ‾‾‾ ‾‾‾.
NWVG CHCUBZTAIR QIY UWI.

Mr. Falcon

John McClane's most famous line in Die Hard 2 — "Yippie-ki-yay, motherfucker"— was changed by American television censors into "Yippie-ki-yay, Mr. Falcon."

NOVEL TERMS

You might find these sex terms and euphemisms in classic and modern books.

```
L  S  Z  N  M  W  W  A  Z  H  U  E  U
A  T  U  X  D  R  K  J  F  O  O  R  X
N  Q  V  Z  O  H  O  N  E  Y  P  O  T
R  U  S  D  O  Q  L  B  I  G  T  G  A
U  U  B  A  H  K  L  A  T  S  O  G  K
Q  D  E  C  N  A  R  T  N  E  O  Z  E
E  J  U  A  A  I  R  V  F  C  R  S  C
C  I  G  B  M  T  P  E  S  M  N  T  I
N  Q  I  H  E  B  F  H  B  Q  A  A  V
E  N  I  R  C  S  E  A  W  M  M  F  E
S  B  H  O  Y  A  O  Y  H  D  E  F  R
S  G  Z  D  T  P  I  R  U  S  O  M  C
E  Y  B  H  G  P  R  E  W  O  L  F  F
```

Crevice	Manhood	Rosebud
Entrance	Manroot	Shaft
Essence	Member	Sheath
Flower	Nub	Staff
Honeypot	Rod	Stalk

POETIC PROFANITY

These alliterative and rhythmic words are sure
to make you orgasm with delight when you find them.

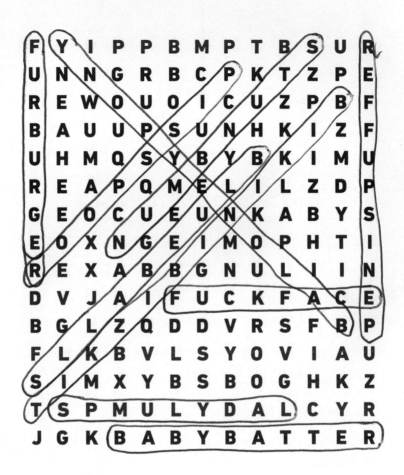

F	Y	I	P	P	B	M	P	T	B	S	U	R
U	N	N	G	R	B	C	P	K	T	Z	P	E
R	E	W	O	U	O	I	C	U	Z	P	B	F
B	A	U	U	P	S	U	N	H	K	I	Z	F
U	H	M	Q	S	Y	B	Y	B	K	I	M	U
R	E	A	P	Q	M	E	L	I	L	Z	D	P
G	E	O	C	U	E	U	N	K	A	B	Y	S
E	O	X	N	G	E	I	M	O	P	H	T	I
R	E	X	A	B	B	G	N	U	L	I	I	N
D	V	J	A	I	F	U	C	K	F	A	C	E
B	G	L	Z	Q	D	D	V	R	S	F	B	P
F	L	K	B	V	L	S	Y	O	V	I	A	U
S	I	M	X	Y	B	S	B	O	G	H	K	Z
T	S	P	M	U	L	Y	D	A	L	C	Y	R
J	G	K	B	A	B	Y	B	A	T	T	E	R

Baby Batter
Baloney Pony
Bikini Bizkit
Blue Balls
Fuckface

Furburger
Lady Lumps
Numbnuts
Penis Puffer
Piss-Poor

TOUGH SHIT ...

... if you don't like this puzzle.

T   O   U   G   H

_ _ _ _ _
(Change one letter)

_ _ _ _
(Remove one letter)

_ _ _ _
(Change one letter)

_ _ _ _
(Change one letter)

_ _ _ _
(Change one letter)

_ _ _ _
(Anagram)

S   H   I   T
(Change one letter)

Clues
(in no particular order)

Cry of pain

Closed tightly

Look but don't ____

Buttocks

Iditarod command

"Thank you very ____!"

PISS & BREATH
Something stinks around here.

P I S S

▼

_ _ _ _
(Change one letter)

▼

_ _ _ _
(Change one letter)

▼

_ _ _ _
(Change one letter)

▼

_ _ _ _ _
(Add one letter)

▼

_ _ _ _ _
(Change one letter)

▼

_ _ _ _ _
(Change one letter)

▼

_ _ _ _ _ _
(Add one letter)

▼

B R E A T H
(Change one letter)

**Clues
(in no particular order)**

BDSM restraint, maybe

Glasgow girl

Whale's leap

Dissolve by percolation

Quarterback's throw

Flog with a whip

____ around (considerate act)

ARCHAIC ASSHOLES

These are slightly more quaint terms for being an idiot.

```
X O T N O O R T L O P T R
A C E P B T D Y V J F O E
R D L I D N Q T H M L M M
N N R L Q O K O Y Y A F M
P S A L T I M B A N C O A
C O V O B L O E I I N O H
O X S C F L P Z P N O L Y
K R N K E U O O H R O W N
I N O O L C L N W J M O N
G A A C A I T I F F I A I
Z D R V W D M A I N S E N
H D V A E Q U N O J C P N
D R A T S A D R D M L L K
```

Bezonian   Ninnyhammer

Caitiff   Pillock

Cullion   Poltroon

Dastard   Ronion

Knave   Saltimbanco

Milksop   Tomfool

Mooncalf   Varlet

CZECH INSULT

Write the name that answers each clue. Then black out each letter in these answers in the random list of letters on the next page. What remains is an English translation of the Czech insult *Vykuř mi!*

1. Actor in *Seven* (1995), *Fight Club* (1999), and *Ocean's Eleven* (2001)

_ _ _ _ _ _ _ _

2. Actor in *Ant-Man* (2015), *Anchorman* (2004), and *The 40-Year-Old Virgin* (2005)

_ _ _ _ _ _ _ _

No romping in the grass

In the 14th century, a mischievous (and horny) Englishman might gauge a lady's sexual interest by verbally offering her a "green gown." If you've ever gotten grass stains on your clothes after an outdoor romp, you'll understand that reference!

BSAMUOD

PKDETRI

RMPATYB

ATLCIUP

IOAPCPK

QUEBEC CUSSES

Pardon our French, but can you find these insults *en français*?

```
E  V  O  J  R  F  V  U  I  J  V  B  P
R  K  A  N  R  A  B  A  T  P  N  Â  K
I  V  S  Y  E  T  E  O  I  F  A  U  N
A  I  E  W  V  M  R  C  N  A  U  C  B
V  A  X  Z  I  R  Ê  I  I  O  W  C  V
L  R  Y  T  I  E  G  T  S  L  T  Ê  J
A  G  S  E  N  M  A  B  P  S  Â  O  Ê
C  E  U  N  A  E  J  Â  S  A  I  C  T
J  V  C  U  D  N  U  B  T  H  B  R  L
T  V  D  R  A  Q  E  R  I  O  B  I  C
C  I  A  T  N  E  M  A  R  C  A  S  X
T  M  F  V  Y  N  Â  N  F  W  A  T  H
O  R  S  B  D  R  A  T  Â  B  C  Â  V
```

Baptême	*Marde*
Bâtard	*Maudit*
Cálice	*Sacrament*
Calvaire	*Tabarnak*
Ciboire	*Torrieu*
Criss	*Toton*
Esti	*Viarge*

CLASSIC OATHS

These are the words you turn to when all the others fail.

N X U A Q C V T U L S S M
Q A U H O J J D A Z R B I
Q F A C H E A M T J U M Y
J H K L E R R D O U C H E
F R O H N B W N M N C E C
U T V N I O D B F L M L X
C X W T J W Q R F G I O P
K L C A X Z P J A S E H I
C H R W T Y T K H T H S S
U I A V K L B I J I S S S
D K P C T R T I Q J I A R
F Y I T D A M N T W F Z B
N D Z D H W W E Y F P B X

Asshole	Dick
Bastard	Douche
Bitch	Fuck
Cock	Piss
Crap	Shit
Damn	Slut
Darn	Twat

GEORGE CARLIN

Other lessons are more enlightening.

	T		P		I			N				A	L			
L	Y	S	U		T		T	L	C	R		O	E			
L	L	M	O	L	T		T	S	E	E	T	T	L	L	B	H
S	I	F	E	I	G	N	A	S	L	Y	O	H	O	U	Y	C
U	I	O	H	U	E	E	O	H	C	H	E	Y	E	A	C	U

Shit.

The first scripted US television show that included an uncensored "shit" was Chicago Hope. That episode aired on October 14, 1999.

JIM C. HINES

This isn't a fantasy novel. It's reality.

DIRTY-SOUNDING ANIMALS

Don't let these zoology words get you too excited.

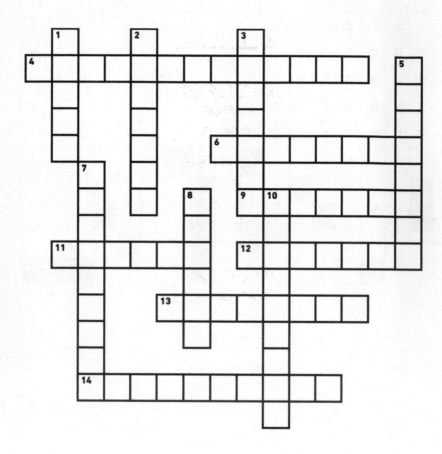

5 LETTERS
BOOBY

6 LETTERS
BEAVER

TURDUS

7 LETTERS
CRAPPIE

JACKASS

PEACOCK

SHIH TZU

8 LETTERS
FARTULUM

PUSSYCAT

TITMOUSE

9 LETTERS
BUGERANUS

HORNY TOAD

10 LETTERS
SPERM WHALE

13 LETTERS
COCKER SPANIEL

BADONKADONK
More cushion for the pushin'!
Find these synonyms for booty.

O C M D M R A E R T O Y S
K R A U N D U C U Z K P S
U W M B B I H S Q N M J A
T U C H U S H G C U T G M
J R I O E Y O E R M R W E
Q E O E G I A D B S M S P
X H K I C T N V B L Y S F
J K M C R K V I N X G K Z
I N F N U E Y K E L I E S
A U I B M X T G L U T E S
N R U Y G N W S S I A H Y
T T S U X P L J O S I C F
I H R E Z N M V N P L Q E

Arse   Posterior
Ass   Rear
Behind   Rump
Bum   Tail
Cheeks   Trunk
Glutes   Tuchus
Heinie   Tushy

WORDOKU

USE THESE LETTERS: **K U W C A F O N G**

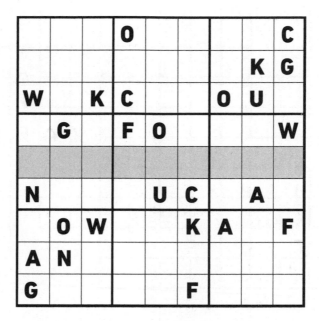

Handy Diagram

pain felt

"duck" "fuck"

A scientific paper published in 2009 showed that swearing does in fact reduce the sensation of pain.

SHIZNIT

Plop these poop phrases into their proper places.

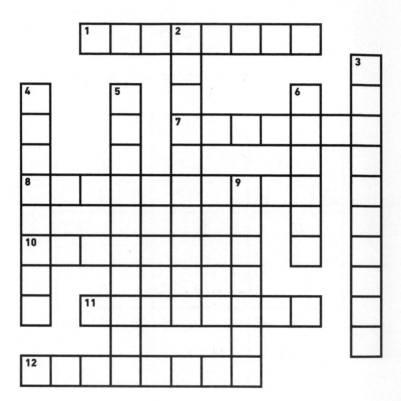

6 LETTERS
Shitty

7 LETTERS
Eat shit

Hot shit

8 LETTERS
Bullshit

Deep shit

Holy shit

Shit list

Shitshow

10 LETTERS
Diddly-shit

Little shit

Load of shit

Pile of shit

HOLY
@#$%&!

Holy @#$%&! A random string of symbols used to represent profanity is called a "grawlix."

HIDDEN ASSES

All these words have an ass snuck in them.
Put them where they belong.

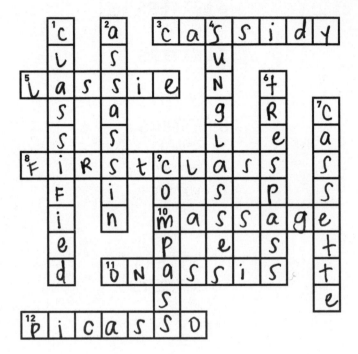

6 LETTERS
~~LASSIE~~

7 LETTERS
~~CASSIDY~~

~~COMPASS~~

~~MASSAGE~~

~~ONASSIS~~

~~PICASSO~~

8 LETTERS
~~ASSASSIN~~

~~CASSETTE~~

~~TRESPASS~~

10 LETTERS
~~CLASSIFIED~~

~~FIRST CLASS~~

~~SUNGLASSES~~

ROBERT DOWNEY JR.

We think Iron Man would feel the same way.

BANKSY

England's notorious graffiti artist
destroys conventional artistic wisdom.

WORDOKU

USE THESE LETTERS: **C A R M G W I N O**

		G	W	M		C	
			I			A	
R							W
G	W	N		A	C		I
	O		I	G		C	W	M
C							A
	G			M			
	M		C	R	O		

Most Profane 2013

A 2013 study showed that Ohioans used profanity more frequently than natives of any other state. (A surprise: Those living in Washington, DC, swore the least.)

RAYLAN GIVENS

Elmore Leonard's fictional deputy US marshal has wise words for buttheads who butt heads.

```
__ ___ ___ ____ __ _____
LC NGD ADJ LJQG PJ PHHEGRY

__ ___ _____' ___ ___ ____
LJ QEY TGAJLJU, NGD APJ LJQG

__ _____' __ ____ _____
PJ PHHEGRY. LC NGD ADJ LJQG PHHEGRYH

___ ___, ___'__ ___ _____.
PRR BPN, NGD'AY QEY PHHEGRY.
```

FREDDIE MERCURY

The Queen has spoken!

```
_'_ ____ __ ___ ____ ___ ____ __
A'F DECV XZ NRT CRXM GON MHVC EU

_____ _____' _____ ___ ____'
HYHWK FNWZAZM, CPWXVPOHC OAC OHXT,

___ _____ ____ __ _____ __ ____.
XZT GNZTHWC GOXV OH GXZVC VN IEPQ.
```

WORDOKU

USE THESE LETTERS: **U E K G F C I P R**

	P		G					K
		F		P		U		C
			R			F		E
						I	C	U
			I	K	C			
I	C	E						
F		P			E			
C		U		R			P	
G					P		E	

There is a small village just outside Salzburg, Austria, called "Fucking." Town signs sporting the name were stolen so frequently by tourists that in 2005, local officials replaced all of them with theft-resistant versions using welded steel and concrete.

LEWIS BLACK
Who knew that astronomy could be funny?

```
____  __  __  __  ____  __  ____  __  ___  ___
KSZI  PY  MB  NB  YMFF  PY  BINC  NX  PMW  PUX

_____  ___.  __  ___  ___  _____  _____
BDKZNSF  UST.  UK  SWK  SFF  BINCCT  FNCCFK

_____  _____  __  ___  _____.
BXPUYFSAKB  OSXZNXR  NX  CIK  MXNHKWBK.
```

MEL BROOKS
He calls 'em like he sees 'em.

```
_'__  ____  _____  __  _____.
F'RV  MVVO  YDDXGVB  UH  RXNEYAFPJ.

_  ___  ____'_  _____.
F  GYJ  PIYP'G  MXNNGIFP.
```

GERMAN INSULT

Use the provided key to decode the English-language translation of this German insult:
Du bist ein arschgeficktes Suppenhuhn!

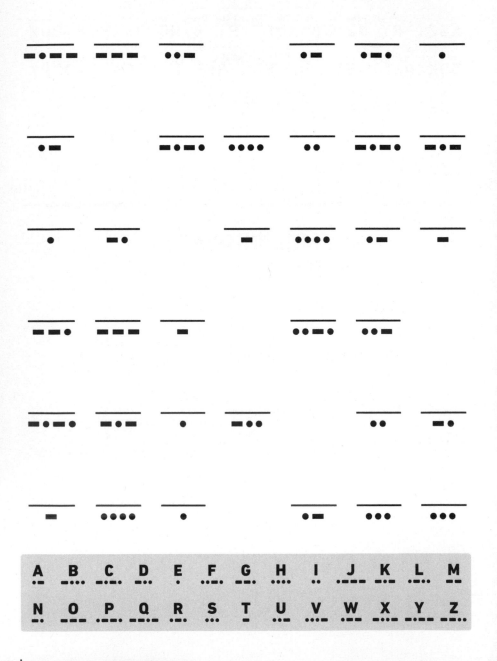

TIM WIGGINS

Stop, drop, but don't roll around in this quote.

```
 _____  _____  _____
WRWHMGKJM  TBHHFWQ  BHKVXJ
 ____  __  ____.  ___  ___  _____
GBEQ  KN  QOFZ.  MKV  TBX  WFZOWH
 __  _____  _____  __  _____
IWBRW  ZOKQW  GWOFXJ  KH  QZΓXC
 ___  ___  ____  __  ____  ____.
NKH  ZOW  HWQZ  KN  MKVH  IFNW.
```

LET'S TALK ABOUT BUTTS
callipygian   having a beautiful rear end
steatopygian   having a prominent rear end
dasypygian   having a hairy rear end
spheropygian   having a very round rear end
pygobombes   people with
well-rounded rear ends
pygoscopophobia   pathological fear
of one's rear end being watched

REFLECTIVE REBUS
Hold this book up to a mirror if you need help with this.

ass

ANGELINA JOLIE
Who can argue with this actress's words?

```
__  _____  ____  __  _____
CH  KQCEJ  BXEQ  CB  GWCETCEJ
_____'_  _____  _____  ____
GWQAQ'B  BPNQGWCEJ  MAPEJ  MCGW
_____  _____,  _'_  _____  __
KQCEJ  YCHHQAQEG,  C'Y  AXGWQA  KQ
_____  _____  _____.
ZPNUFQGQFD  HIZTCEJ  NQEGXF.
```

CHINESE INSULT

Use the provided key to decode the English-language translation of this Chinese insult:
Cao ni zuzong shiba dai!

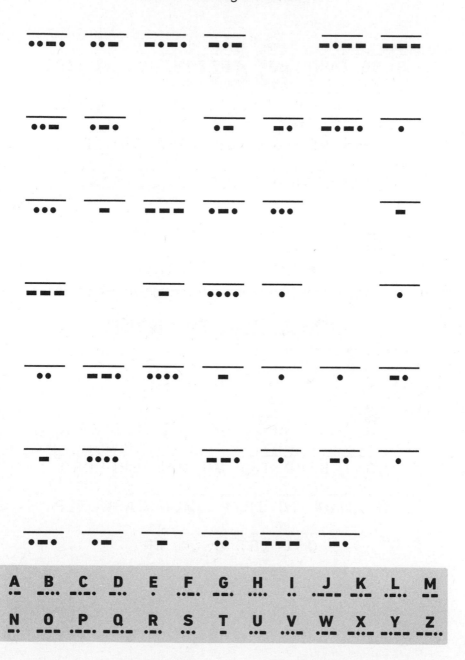

A	B	C	D	E	F	G	H	I	J	K	L	M
.-	-...	-.-.	-..	.	..-.	--.	....	..	.---	-.-	.-..	--

N	O	P	Q	R	S	T	U	V	W	X	Y	Z
-.	---	.--.	--.-	.-.	...	-	..-	...-	.--	-..-	-.--	--..

DEB CALETTI

This young adult writer knows about safety in numbers.

```
____ _____,’ _____ ___,’ __ ___
SENG CVHUVBJ, TDZIG TUU, VC ZRI

____ _____ _____ __ ___ _____
EBUS EZRIG LIGCEB VB ZRI AEGUO

___ _____ ___ _____
ARE NBOIGCZTBOC REA DNPYIO

__ ____ _____ ____ ___.
NL SENG LTGIBZC FTOI SEN.
```

JONATHAN FRANZEN

You can't argue with the author's über-truism.

```
___ ___ _____ _____ ___ ____
WAL RQL WAMQZ QRFRCI USQ WSNL

____ ____ ___ __ ___ _____
SOSI BPRD IRT MH WAL BPLLCRD

__ ____ __ ____ ____ _____
WR BTUN TG IRTP JMBL OASWLXLP

___ ___ ____ __.
OSI IRT OSQW WR.
```

ERICA JONG

Chaos, though, is often a sign of genius.

	N	S		J	O	S	E			R								K
I	M	G	A	A	G	F					H	I	N			C	T	I
F	U	A	N	U	A	T		L		R	O	F	F	S	N	U	O	O
T	L	E	I	D	N	L	E		T	T	Y	N	I	F		D	C	N
I	M	I	N	L	I	M	Y	T	I	W	I	I	G		C		A	N

DANIEL RADCLIFFE

Who knew that Harry Potter could curse like a sailor?

```
_ ____ __ __ ____-_____ _____
M GRXC HL TX RXYK-ALPRAMLGR ITLGH

__ _____, ___ ____ _ _____,
UF WXMJWH, TGH HWXP M HWLGJWH,

____ ____, _'_ _____ _____.
KGAV HWIH, M'U WIDDF BLHHXD.
```

First in
1889
"Motherfucker"

The earliest recorded usage of "motherfucker" comes from an 1889 Texas murder trial, during which the victim reportedly referred to the defendant as a "God damned mother-fucking, bastardly son-of-a-bitch" just before he died.

CHRIS ROCK

Season your life with the comedian's words.

```
_____ __ _____ __ ____ ____.
JYXHUHAT HT ZAVHYBN HZ XHQY ZCXB.

_ _____ ___ __ ____, ___ ___ ____
C XHBBXY FHB HZ UAAP, FKB BAA RKVL

____ ____ __ ____ ____.
DHXX WKVQ KG NAKJ WAAP.
```

PICTURESQUE PICTOGRAM

Some people are just creative in all the wrong ways.

LARS ULRICH

Let this keep drumming into your head.

J.A. KONRATH

No wonder he writes thriller and horror books.

___ __ ___ _____ _____
KXW KY PVW BAWDPWIP FKGAXWNI

__ ____ __ _____ _____
CX MCYW CI KTWAOKZCXB CXIWOGACPN

___ _____ __ _____ ___
DXS MWDAXCXB PK PAGMN XKP

____ _ ____.
BCTW D IVCP.

JOHNNY DEPP

Captain Jack Sparrow approves of this message.

____ ____ _____ _____ ___
DKFU ELLS OJCPIT BJNRGNZ GIZ

_____ ____ _ ____ _____
ZJI'U TPCL G FWPU GHJKU

____ _____ _____.
RWGU GIXHJZX UWPIEF.

__ ____ ___ ____ __ ___
ZJ RWGU XJK WGCL UJ ZJ-

___ ___.
BJN XJK.

WORDOKU

		E					K	
A				D		O		B
	H			B	S	N		
B			N					
		S	K		O	N		
				H				S
	O	B	A				H	
N		D		E				K
	K				E			

WORDOKU

USE THESE LETTERS: **D A R I T B H S E**

		D		H		R		I
	A		H	E				
	R			B				
R	E				I			
I								H
		H				E	T	
		B				T		
		S	A		D			
T		E			S			

ERNEST CLINE

That escalated quickly, but maybe that's to be expected from the *Ready Player One* author.

ANTHONY BOURDAIN

When you're successful, you can make the rules.

‾ ‾‾‾‾ ‾‾ ‾‾‾‾ ‾‾‾ ‾‾‾‾‾‾‾‾‾ ‾‾ ‾‾ ‾‾‾‾
D MKQY YR ZNNG YFN KOOFRSNO DQ JT SDIN

‾‾ ‾‾ ‾‾‾‾‾‾‾‾ ‾‾‾‾‾‾‾, ‾‾ ‾‾‾ ‾‾‾‾.
YR KQ KVORSLYN JDQDJLJ, DI QRY XNER.

‾‾‾‾'‾ ‾‾‾‾‾ ‾‾‾‾', ‾‾‾‾ ‾‾‾‾‾‾‾
YFKY'O MREYF ENKS, ENKS JRQNT—

‾‾ ‾‾‾ ‾‾‾‾ ‾‾‾‾‾‾‾‾ ‾‾ ‾‾‾‾ ‾‾‾‾.
YR QRY FKAN KOOFRSNO DQ TRLE SDIN.

CONNER SMITH

How you feel is often all about perspective.

```
___  ___  _____  ____  _____  ____
XYL  RDA  NWHAV  XYLF  ZCYSH  SOPH

_____  ____  _____  ____
SYYBOAM  VYZA  DIYOVOAM  NCOE

__  ___  _____  ____  ____  __
YF  XYL  RYLSV  GLNE  SYYB  LW

___  ___  ____  _  ____.
DAV  AYE  MOIH  D  VDJA.
```

WIZ KHALIFA

The rapper will help you find your way to the street.

```
_  ___,_  _____  _____  _____.
W  RYH'V  ZEKIX  KPVXF  KHLYHX.

__  ___  ____  ____  ___  __
WP  LYA  NKHHK  NKSD  YAV  YP  UL

____,  ____  _  __  ____  ___
SWPX,  VEXH  W'SS  EYSR  VEX

_____  ____  ____  ___  ___.
PAZDWHT  RYYF  YOXH  PYF  LYA.
```

ROBERT PLANT

The King *did* cause different responses from admirers.

		L		N												
E		E	V	I	C		W	L				D				H
H	L	W	F	E	D		K	N		A		A		O	U	T
A	E	S	R	S	G		E	I	E	W	T	H	A	T	O	A
T	E	L	A	W	E	K	L	R	S	E	N	A	B	M	H	A
T	T	R	A	U	S	A	L	A	K	T	H	A	T	T	M	T
			■			■					■					
■						■				■					■	
	■					■					■		■			
									■				■			
	■				■				■					■		
						■	■	■	■	■	■	■	■	■	■	■

ERNEST HEMINGWAY

It's not easy becoming a world-famous writer.

M PEMVD XQD WRLD XC

NRAVDEWMDTD VX QMQDVB-XQD

WRLDA XC AYMV. M VEB VX WSV

VYD AYMV MQ VYD PRAVDJRAIDV.

The first use of the word "fuck" in any major American film was in M*A*S*H (1970), directed by Robert Altman.

GEORGE CARLIN

Need another Carlin witticism for your collection?

```
 __ ___ ____ __ ____,
 IK OFG VSXA IK JCP'A PKKJ
 ____ ____ __ ___,_
 IXAS YCPKG IK JCP'A SNRK
 __ _____ _____ __ ___,_ ____.
 AC XYTLKVV TKCTHK IK JCP'A HXWK.
```

PHILIP LARKIN

This quote from the British poet
has a phrase that rhymes with "suck off."

```
 _____ __ _____,_ _____
 JWXZUC FV OWDWRC'V DQVFOXVV
 _____ ___ ____,_ _
 XKNXJZ ZGX JWXZ'V—
 ___ _____ ____ ___ ____ ___.
 HOR XMXUCDWRC XSVX NHO PQNA WPP.
```

GREEK INSULT

Write the word that answers all three clues. Then black
out each letter in this answer in the random list
of letters on the next page. What remains is
an English translation of the Greek insult
Na mou klaseis ta'rxidia!

1. Took part in BDSM, maybe
2. Word with pussy or cream
3. Thoroughly defeated

_ _ _ _ _ _ _

DFWAIE

IRDTPD

HOPINH

MEHYBW

PHAILW

PDLSWI

CHERYL STRAYED

You sometimes just have to get *Wild* with life.

```
___  ____  _____  ___  ___
BEO  JOQB  BECML  UGA  IPM

_____  __  ____  ____  ____
HGQQCJZU  VG  NCBE  UGAF  ZCKO

__  __  _____  ___  _____
CQ  BG  BPITZO  BEO  WGBEOFKAITCML

____  ___  __  __.
QECB  GAB  GK  CB.
```

MERLIN MANN

In other words, everyone's got one.

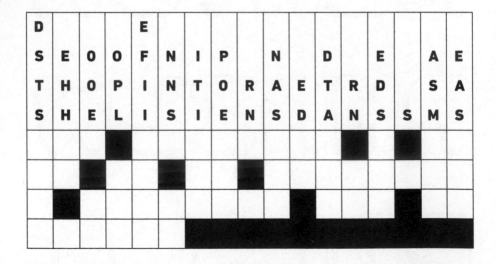

NEVILLE FLYNN

When you've had it, you've had it. Open a window!

_____ __ _____!
GBEYKR VA GBEYKR!

_ ____ ___ __ ____ _____
V RNOG RNC VI UVIR IRGAG

_____ _____
LEIRGJDYQSVBK ABNSGA

__ ____ _____ _____!
EB IRVA LEIRGJDYQSVBK XTNBG!

_____ _____ __. _'_ _____
GOGJWZECW AIJNX VB. V'L NZEYI

__ ____ ____ _____ _____.
IE EXGB AELG DYQSVBK UVBCEUA.

RUDY FRANCISCO

Raise a glass to this poet's wise words.

```
      __  _____ '_  _____  __  ___  _____  __  ____
      WB  TMPRK'B  NLBBPI  WX  BYP  CVLRR  WR  YLVX

      ____  __  ____  _____ _ _____ '_  _____  __
      XJVV  MI  YLVX  PNGBD—BYPIP'R  ULBPI  WK

      ___  ___ .  _____  ____  ____
      BYP  EJG .  TIWKF  BYLB  RYWB

      ___  ____  _____ .
      LKT  RBMG  EMNGVLWKWKC .
```

DAVID SEDARIS

You checked your *Merriam-Webster*, didn't you?

```
      __  ___ '__  _____  ___  _____ '
      RE  GHP'WK  YHHIRJV  EHW  NGTADSZG ,

      ___ '__  ____  __  _____  ____
      GHP'YY  ERJC  RS  LKSFKKJ  NZRS

      ___  _____  __  ___  _____ .
      DJC  NGAZRYRN  RJ  SZK  CROSRHJDWG .
```

CONOR McGREGOR

He doesn't care about bashing his opponents either.

E			A		G											
S			I	A	N	S				E	A					I
I	H	L	I	M	P	L	Y	K		P	O	O	T		G	H
E	E	T	R	N	F	H	C	E	S	A	A	N	U	T	T	F
V	E	S	M	U	T	U	W	I	M	D	B	N	K	I	R	I

DYLAN MORAN

Check the menu description before making a decision.

```
_____  ___  ___  _____  _____.
EIGIJ  QJA  QBI  VYMRV  QBFEK.
                      '      ___?
___  ____  ___  __'_  _____?
AYO  UEYH  HBA  FQ'Z  VYMRV?
_____  __'_  ____-
XIMROZI  FQ'Z  ZBFQ—
____'_  ___  __'_  _____.
QBRQ'Z  HBA  FQ'Z  VYMRV.
```

PITCHER PICTOGRAM

Knock this one out of the park!

DOWN-AND-OUT REBUS

It's probably sticking to your shoes now.

___

THE WALKING DEAD'S BUD

Christopher Berry's character knows you can't hesitate.

```
__ ___ ____ __ ___ ____',
LY GTK SUOX DT XUD WSLD,

____ ___ __ _____.
MXWD JTD DT JLMMAX.

____', ____', _____, _____.
MLDX,  ZSXN,  WNUAATN,  HXCXUD.

__ ____ _____.
LD BTXW PKLZRXH.
```

GILLIAN FLYNN

You don't have to go to *Dark Places* to solve this puzzle.

```
 _   __  ___  _____  __  ___  __  _____
 S  BL  VUH  BVMEG  UE  IBR  UE  KBCCG
__  ___  ___.  _  _____  ___  ____  _  ____.
HU  IXX  GUO.  S  WUOYR  VUH  MSTX  B  IKSH.
___  ___'_  ____  _____.
GUO  RUV'H  XTXV  ESCCYX.
```

A.S. KING

This author knows what you don't want to be.

```
___  _____  __  ____  __  _____.
SRQ  KIFXT  CU  YAXX  IY  GUURIXQU.
____  ___  ___  _____  __  ____  ____
KRGS  GFQ  HIA  TICBJ  SI  WGDQ  UAFQ
___'__  ___  ___  __  ____?
HIA'FQ  BIS  IBQ  IY  SRQW?
```

BULGARIAN INSULT

Use the provided key to decode the English-language translation of this Bulgarian insult:

Kon da ti go natrese!

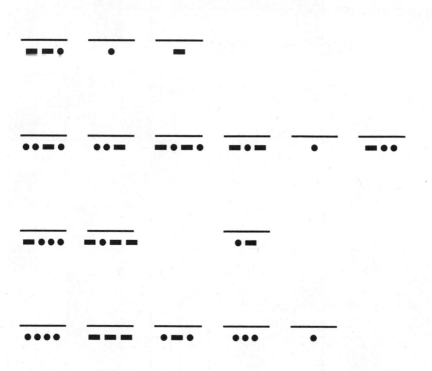

A	B	C	D	E	F	G	H	I	J	K	L	M
.-	-...	-.-.	-..	.	..-.	--.	....	..	.---	-.-	.-..	--

N	O	P	Q	R	S	T	U	V	W	X	Y	Z
-.	---	.--.	--.-	.-.	...	-	..-	...-	.--	-..-	-.--	--..

OUR ORIGINS

Who *really* rules the animal kingdom?

$\overline{104}\ \overline{39}\ \overline{76}\ \overline{17}\ \overline{40}\ \overline{67}\ \overline{63}\ \overline{165}\ \overline{37}\ \overline{170}\ \overline{177}$
Author of the quote

$\overline{168}\ \overline{8}\ \overline{144}\ \overline{152}\ \overline{150}\ \overline{25}\ \overline{116}\ \overline{137}\ \overline{123}\ \overline{19}\ \overline{24}\ \overline{1}\ \overline{166}\ \overline{60}$
Certain sideshow performer

$\overline{11}\ \overline{15}\ \overline{95}\ \overline{5}\ \overline{92}\ \overline{136}\ \overline{73}\ \overline{18}\ \overline{83}\ \overline{6}\ \overline{131}$
2017 role for Gal Gadot

$\overline{164}\ \overline{84}\ \overline{146}\ \overline{118}\ \overline{140}\ \overline{149}\ \overline{32}\ \overline{10}\ \overline{81}\ \overline{138}\ \overline{74}\ \overline{142}\ \overline{41}\ \overline{174}\ \overline{153}\ \overline{34}\ \overline{100}\ \overline{145}$
Actress married to Michael Douglas

$\overline{108}\ \overline{80}\ \overline{22}\ \overline{66}\ \overline{78}\ \overline{46}\ \overline{45}\ \overline{159}\ \overline{109}\ \overline{16}\ \overline{27}\ \overline{71}$
"Kokomo" and "Good Vibrations" band

$\overline{156}\ \overline{70}\ \overline{28}\ \overline{143}\ \overline{20}\ \overline{30}\ \overline{139}\ \overline{135}\ \overline{26}\ \overline{105}\ \overline{169}\ \overline{90}\ \overline{176}$
King Tut process

$\overline{56}\ \overline{50}\ \overline{75}\ \overline{9}\ \overline{99}\ \overline{54}\ \overline{86}\ \overline{126}\ \overline{64}\ \overline{175}\ \overline{77}\ \overline{47}\ \overline{157}\ \overline{65}\ \overline{172}\ \overline{57}\ \overline{51}$
2005–2014 sitcom with Neil Patrick Harris

$\overline{124}\ \overline{125}\ \overline{161}\ \overline{91}\ \overline{98}\ \overline{102}\ \overline{106}\ \overline{115}\ \overline{122}\ \overline{4}\ \overline{21}\ \overline{29}$
Star of Bugsy and Bonnie and Clyde

$\overline{111}\ \overline{133}\ \overline{58}\ \overline{141}\ \overline{23}\ \overline{179}\ \overline{85}\ \overline{68}\ \overline{62}\ \overline{173}\ \overline{130}\ \overline{49}\ \overline{3}\ \overline{2}$
Cheetos's feline mascot

$\overline{96}\ \overline{97}\ \overline{94}\ \overline{36}\ \overline{119}\ \overline{113}\ \overline{7}\ \overline{154}\ \overline{127}$
Roget's reference

$\overline{171}\ \overline{43}\ \overline{33}\ \overline{103}\ \overline{89}$
Short social media post

$\overline{79}\ \overline{87}\ \overline{155}\ \overline{14}\ \overline{129}\ \overline{38}$
Family jewels

$\overline{120}\ \overline{69}\ \overline{53}\ \overline{148}\ \overline{160}\ \overline{147}\ \overline{110}\ \overline{59}\ \overline{178}$
Fast-food combo choice

$\overline{88}\ \overline{158}\ \overline{12}\ \overline{61}\ \overline{52}\ \overline{117}\ \overline{114}$
Pigeon perches, often

$\overline{151}\ \overline{93}\ \overline{121}\ \overline{167}\ \overline{112}\ \overline{162}\ \overline{132}\ \overline{48}\ \overline{31}$
Happily _____ (fairy tale ending)

$\overline{82}\ \overline{101}\ \overline{107}\ \overline{42}\ \overline{44}\ \overline{72}\ \overline{35}$
Cooked some onions, say

$\overline{55}\ \overline{163}\ \overline{128}\ \overline{134}\ \overline{13}$
They can be tied

Man's best friend indeed!

_ ____ ___ ___.
A GATB KRB CJE.

__ ___'_ ___ __
AP RB MVI'K BVK AK,

__ ____ __,' __ _____ __ __.
JL PQMT AK, RB NAHHBH JI AK.

_ ___ ___ _____ ____.
A MVI EBK YBRAIC KRVK.

fokken
↰
free tattoo idea

The English word "fuck" is believed to be derived from the Middle Dutch word fokken, which means "to thrust or copulate with."

ED SHEERAN
Measured words from the ginger singer.

```
__ _____ _____ ___
UR KFWJFYJ QJEEK NFM

__ _____ _____,
QF GLTYCJ NFMZKJER,

____ ____ __ ____
QJEE QLJW QF CF RMGX

_____.
QLJWKJEHJK.
```

HENRY MILLER
That will make going to the bathroom that much harder.

```
____ ____ _____ _____,
RQCI ZQGP XCFWTCZ SKVDKXVC,

___ ____ ____ __ ____
PQC UWWL RGVV XC XWLI

_____ _____.
RGPQWDP KZZQWVCZ.
```

AFRIKAANS INSULT

Use the provided key to decode the English-language translation of this Afrikaans insult:

Siug aan my aambeie en wag vir beter dae!

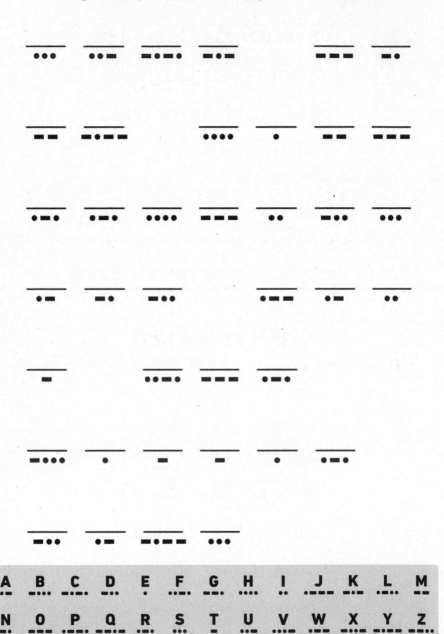

LARRY DAVID

Save those for outdoor adventures.

```
___ ____ ___ _____
FYQ OCYK KZY KJITA
_____ _____?
AQCDPIAAJA GCAGWJ?
_____ __ __
VPGCW NJYNPJ ICW
_____.
IAAZYPJA.
```

TROUBLE A-BREWIN' PICTOGRAM

Even an umbrella might not help.

AMHARIC INSULT

Use the provided key to decode the English-language translation of this Amharic insult: *Silbabot!*

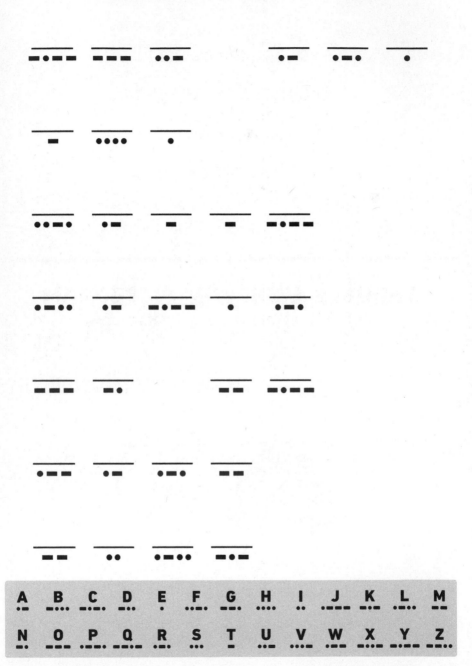

BRET EASTON ELLIS

Life's all about that *American Psycho* perspective.

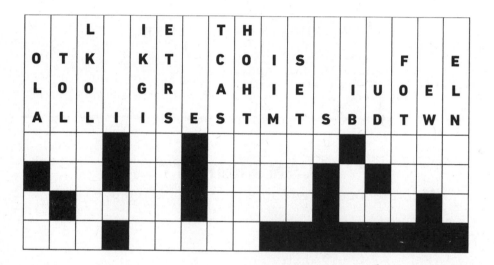

LEWIS BLACK

Did he stutter?

```
__ ___ ____ ____,
FS SGT ACOZ QFXA,
_____ _'__ _____ ___
TJGOG F'EG IFEGH WKO
___ ____, ____ ___'_ ____
XCC ICSB, WYQZ FRS'X GEGS
_ ____-__'_ _ _ _____.
K TCOH—FX'R K QCNNK.
```

ALAN BENNETT

Accurate thought wrought by the English playwright.

```
___ __ C _____
AKQ VK C VONCEO
_____? __'_ ____
ACPUKBX? CU'P IZPU
___ _____ _____
KEO NZSYCEM UACEM
_____ _____.
RNUOB REKUAOB.
```

HENRY ROLLINS

This rocker knows how to roll with the punches.

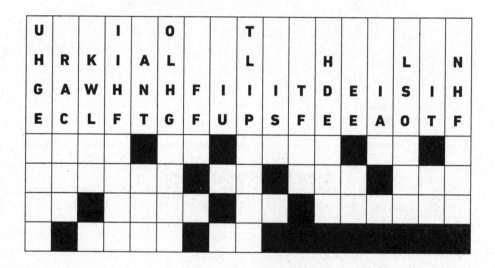

CASUAL PICTOGRAM
Watch out for the splatter.

JIM THOMPSON
You'll need to wear industrial-strength gloves for this.

L	I		D		I	T		E		T	U		K		E	
O	F	F	E		W	I		A		H	H	C	D	E	T	
R	B	E	S	H	I	S	R	W	I	B	A	N	A	L	B	A
			■		■		■									■
	■					■				■		■				
				■			■									■

STEPHEN FRY

Keep your responses short and curt.

TONI MORRISON

You gotta know how to let go.

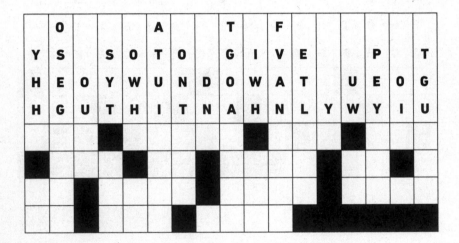

JOAN CRAWFORD

Mommie Dearest says it's time to ride!

GRANDMA'S GEM

Or as Ice Cube said: "You better check
yo self before you wreck yo self."

$\overline{125}\ \overline{93}\ \overline{58}\ \ \overline{124}\ \overline{119}\ \overline{141}\ \overline{48}\ \ \overline{110}\ \overline{73}\ \ \overline{13}\ \ \overline{38}$
Author of the quote

$\overline{68}\ \ \overline{89}\ \ \overline{61}\ \ \overline{50}\ \ \overline{44}\ \ \overline{102}\ \overline{79}\ \ \overline{82}\ \ \overline{70}\ \ \overline{32}\ \ \overline{27}\ \ \overline{135}\ \overline{64}\ \ \overline{132}\ \overline{95}\ \ \overline{47}\ \ \overline{123}\ \overline{28}$
1983 U2 song about a deadly Irish protest

$\overline{90}\ \ \overline{88}\ \ \overline{113}\ \overline{134}\ \overline{22}\ \ \overline{114}\ \overline{37}\ \ \overline{8}\ \ \ \overline{31}\ \ \overline{130}\ \overline{17}$
The _____ Picture Show (1975 musical comedy)

$\overline{69}\ \ \overline{98}\ \ \overline{40}\ \ \overline{20}\ \ \overline{24}\ \ \overline{15}\ \ \overline{9}\ \ \ \overline{10}\ \ \overline{3}$
The _____ Redemption (1994 prison drama)

$\overline{111}\ \overline{120}\ \overline{56}\ \ \overline{128}\ \overline{75}\ \ \overline{92}\ \ \overline{107}\ \overline{26}\ \ \overline{5}\ \ \ \overline{42}\ \ \overline{12}\ \ \overline{25}\ \ \overline{115}\ \overline{84}\ \ \overline{51}\ \ \overline{49}\ \ \overline{140}$
2010 time-travel comedy

$\overline{55}\ \ \overline{103}\ \overline{11}\ \ \overline{46}\ \ \overline{29}\ \ \overline{21}\ \ \overline{122}\ \overline{59}\ \ \overline{99}\ \ \overline{43}\ \ \overline{108}\ \overline{101}\ \overline{87}$
Characteristic of uranium and radon

$\overline{4}\ \ \ \overline{106}\ \overline{133}\ \overline{18}\ \ \overline{81}\ \ \overline{6}\ \ \ \overline{33}\ \ \overline{67}\ \ \overline{80}\ \ \overline{23}$
Koala's food source

$\overline{1}\ \ \ \overline{77}\ \ \overline{142}\ \overline{118}\ \overline{85}\ \ \overline{127}\ \overline{104}\ \overline{16}\ \ \overline{57}\ \ \overline{121}\ \overline{74}\ \ \overline{94}\ \ \overline{131}\ \overline{60}\ \ \overline{62}$
1997 Italian comedy-drama set in WWII

$\overline{139}\ \overline{126}\ \overline{96}\ \ \overline{129}\ \overline{72}\ \ \overline{39}\ \ \overline{86}\ \ \overline{66}\ \ \overline{105}\ \overline{109}$
The power of _____

$\overline{52}\ \ \overline{54}\ \ \overline{35}\ \ \overline{78}\ \ \overline{116}\ \overline{19}\ \ \overline{91}$
US vice president (1977–1981)

$\overline{65}\ \ \overline{137}\ \overline{76}\ \ \overline{63}\ \ \overline{41}\ \ \overline{117}\ \overline{100}\ \overline{36}\ \ \overline{14}\ \ \overline{112}\ \overline{136}\ \overline{30}\ \ \overline{97}$
Like one who avoids black cats and ladders

$\overline{53}\ \ \overline{2}\ \ \ \overline{45}\ \ \overline{7}\ \ \ \overline{138}\ \overline{34}\ \ \overline{71}\ \ \overline{83}$
Plymouth Rock landers

GEORGE CARLIN

That's some serious disgust!

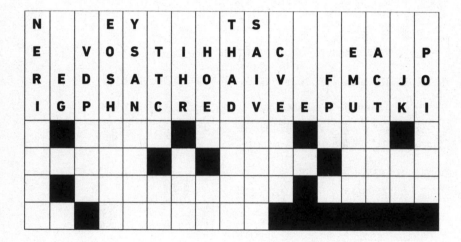

HUNTER S. THOMPSON

There's no middle ground here.

DIRTY-SOUNDING PLACES

Start planning your road trip to these real destinations.

5 LETTERS
Dildo

6 LETTERS
Climax

Hooker

7 LETTERS
Bumpass

Cumming

8 LETTERS
Cockburn

Morehead

9 LETTERS
Moist Cove

10 LETTERS
Humptulips

Middelfart

Shitterton

11 LETTERS
Intercourse

Spread Eagle

12 LETTERS
Tightsqueeze

FUNNY AS ...

It's also a great way to compliment a joke.

$\overline{111}\ \overline{27}\ \overline{45}\ \overline{52}\ \overline{36}\ \overline{60}\ \overline{68}\ \overline{25}\ \overline{102}\ \overline{18}\ \overline{5}\ \ \overline{69}$
Author of the quote

$\overline{107}\ \overline{47}\ \overline{3}\ \ \overline{67}\ \overline{88}\ \overline{87}\ \overline{53}\ \overline{91}\ \overline{112}\ \overline{4}\ \ \overline{43}\ \overline{41}\ \overline{66}\ \overline{93}\ \overline{30}\ \overline{9}\ \ \overline{110}\ \overline{7}\ \ \overline{58}$
Very unlucky day (also the title of a series of horror films)

$\overline{61}\ \overline{71}\ \overline{75}\ \overline{17}\ \overline{51}\ \overline{33}\ \overline{96}\ \overline{83}\ \overline{65}\ \overline{74}\ \overline{114}\ \overline{70}\ \overline{99}\ \overline{44}\ \overline{86}$
What so _____ … (anthem line)

$\overline{2}\ \ \overline{94}\ \overline{22}\ \overline{117}\ \overline{34}\ \overline{98}\ \overline{15}\ \overline{20}\ \overline{50}\ \overline{92}\ \overline{10}\ \overline{81}\ \overline{105}\ \overline{21}$
Like most modern televisions

$\overline{100}\ \overline{23}\ \overline{103}\ \overline{76}\ \overline{12}\ \overline{11}\ \overline{55}\ \overline{113}\ \overline{26}\ \overline{80}\ \overline{63}\ \overline{54}\ \overline{85}\ \overline{115}$
McDonald's, Burger King, Wendy's, etc.

$\overline{64}\ \overline{49}\ \overline{39}\ \overline{82}\ \overline{14}\ \overline{101}$
Grovel

$\overline{29}\ \overline{77}\ \overline{42}\ \overline{104}\ \overline{8}\ \ \overline{109}\ \overline{6}$
Roman god of drunken orgies

$\overline{95}\ \overline{46}\ \overline{31}\ \overline{35}\ \overline{106}\ \overline{57}\ \overline{108}$
2000 "backward" film by Christopher Nolan

$\overline{79}\ \overline{37}\ \overline{118}\ \overline{119}\ \overline{48}\ \overline{40}\ \overline{62}\ \overline{1}$
Snitches get _____

$\overline{16}\ \overline{32}\ \overline{56}\ \overline{19}\ \overline{59}\ \overline{28}\ \overline{90}\ \overline{13}\ \overline{89}$
General agreement

$\overline{116}\ \overline{72}\ \overline{78}\ \overline{73}\ \overline{84}\ \overline{38}\ \overline{24}\ \overline{97}$
Former attorney general Jeff _____ (2017–2018)

JONATHAN WINTERS

Better just use the whole loaf.

ERNEST HEMINGWAY

Papa had his running smoothly.

	T		S			T		R				
L	E		T	O	R	F	O	K		A		O	T		A
T	W	I	I	D	E	S	T	I	S	R		O	G	O	I	D
T	H	R	N	M	T	T	E	C	R	O	S	O	B	F	I	L
H	I	G	I	F	E	H	O	C	E	P	A	E	N	U	O	S

DAVID SEDARIS

It's a sweet approach!

	E	U					I	F				C			G	S	
Y	O	E		C	K	C	L	I		J	U	M	A		A	O	
H	O	U		R	S	S	W	N		S	N	I	E		S	Y	
Y	H	R		F	U	O	K	I	T	G	B	D	E	N	M	T	T
W	F	U		N	D	E	H	T	N	A	O	R	T	N	D	A	Y

ANONYMOUS

But you might still get kicked in the balls.

	N				T	C	S			A					
	L				S	E	H			A		R			A	N
	A	N	A	A	C	O	L	O		S	A		D		I	O	I
I	T	N	B	I	S	S	H	S	C	E	L	I		H	T	T
N	A	O	T	C	S	R	T	S	L	L	O	N	W	T	P	S	R
D	O	L	T	G	E	A	X	I	Y	T	U	L	O	M	E	S

FIRST-WORLD PROBLEMS

This comedian also said fat people don't fail cooking.

1	2		3	4	5		6	7		8	9	10	11	
12	13	14	15		16	17		18	19	20	21	22	23	24
	25	26		27	28		29	30	31	32	33	34	35	36
	37	38		39	40	41	42				43	44	45	46
47	48		49	50	51	52	53	54		55	56	57		58
	59	60	61	62	63	64	65	66		67	68		69	70
71	72		73	74	75		76	77	78	79	80		81
82	83	84	85	86		87	88		89	90	91	92	93	94
	95		96	97	98		99		100	101	102	103	104	105
106		107	108	109	110	111	112	113		114	115	116	117	118
119	120	121	122	123	124								

102 70 21 22 95 120 38 66 80
Author of the quote

29 85 83 25 91 73 48 14 44 1 99 105 116 71 5
1980 hit song by Journey

12 2 108 33 94 79 42 60 74 24 110 77 87 82 3
_____ in Las Vegas (1998 film starring Johnny Depp)

31 62 111 45 18 27 15 7 93 78 23 55 49 63 114 97
He was "Jack" to Kate Winslet's "Rose" in Titanic

46 124 40 47 96 113 123 81 89 30 16 57
He wrote the "Seven Words You Can Never Say on Television"

109 101 36 103 51 68 69 115 26 112 76
One Flew Over the _____ (1975 film)

13 52 67 56 10 59 53 65 118 107 9 6 104 4 88
Visual paradox

20 58 84 75 100 39 119 54
Crawfish _____ (Cajun specialty)

64 41 98 11 121 19
_____ City (Batman's home)

G E N T L E M E N
106 50 122 72 61 32 8 86 17
_____ Prefer Blondes (1953 film)

G O N E W I T H
34 117 92 28 90 35 37 43
_____ the Wind (1939 film)

POLISH INSULT

Write the word that answers all three clues. Then black out each letter in this answer in the random list of letters on the next page. What remains is an English translation of the Polish insult *Jebiesz jeze!*

1. Southern capital
2. Olympic host city in 1996
3. 2016 television series created by Donald Glover

_ _ _ _ _ _ _

TYAOLT
UATFAU
NCKHNT
ELDLGN
ELHLAQ
NLTGAS

CHUCK WENDIG

Followers of the Terribleminds blog will appreciate this.

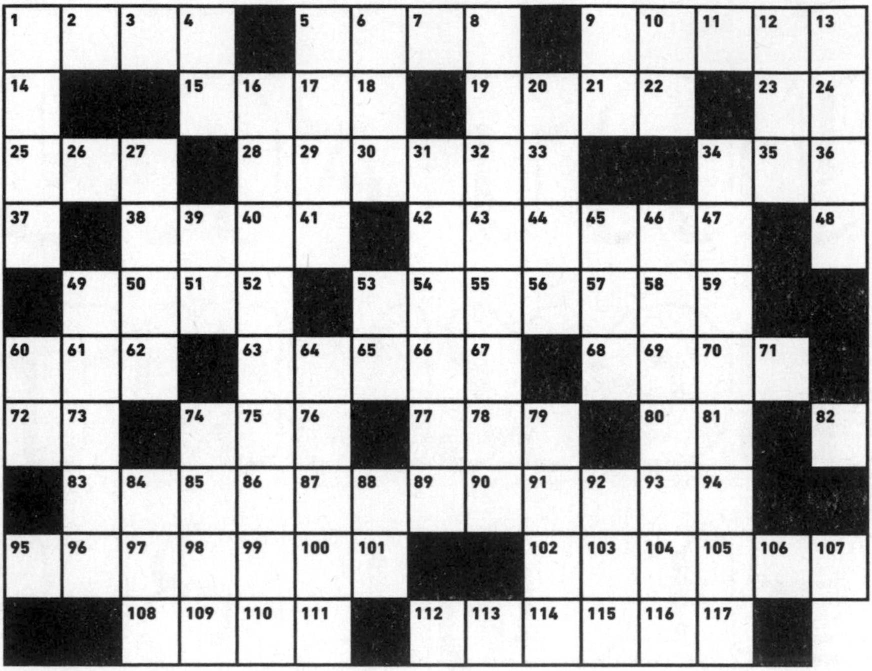

Most Profane
2017

A 2017 study found that people from Virginia used curse words more frequently than those from any other state. (Hawaiians cursed the least.)

$\overline{4}$ $\overline{84}$ $\overline{88}$ $\overline{54}$ $\overline{47}$ $\overline{57}$ $\overline{112}$ $\overline{5}$ $\overline{42}$ $\overline{18}$ $\overline{111}$ $\overline{93}$ $\overline{83}$ $\overline{31}$ $\overline{110}$
Satirist songwriter who wrote "Amish Paradise" and "Eat It"

$\overline{102}$ $\overline{115}$ $\overline{87}$ $\overline{21}$ $\overline{107}$ $\overline{53}$ $\overline{67}$ $\overline{89}$ $\overline{66}$ $\overline{82}$ $\overline{113}$ $\overline{33}$
British comedian and creator of "The Office"

$\overline{24}$ $\overline{12}$ $\overline{94}$ $\overline{65}$ $\overline{117}$ $\overline{16}$ $\overline{29}$ $\overline{114}$ $\overline{48}$
Infamous bombing target of 1945

$\overline{81}$ $\overline{98}$ $\overline{14}$ $\overline{116}$ $\overline{50}$ $\overline{56}$ $\overline{52}$ $\overline{92}$ $\overline{75}$ $\overline{27}$ $\overline{108}$ $\overline{45}$ $\overline{43}$ $\overline{10}$ $\overline{3}$ $\overline{7}$ $\overline{63}$
Street racing film series, with "The"

$\overline{104}$ $\overline{58}$ $\overline{6}$ $\overline{9}$ $\overline{28}$ $\overline{77}$ $\overline{8}$ $\overline{78}$ $\overline{49}$ $\overline{25}$ $\overline{35}$ $\overline{32}$
A day late and _____

$\overline{79}$ $\overline{86}$ $\overline{72}$ $\overline{38}$ $\overline{39}$ $\overline{62}$ $\overline{60}$ $\overline{1}$ $\overline{44}$ $\overline{74}$ $\overline{36}$
Mount Rushmore's state

$\overline{34}$ $\overline{96}$ $\overline{68}$ $\overline{64}$ $\overline{40}$ $\overline{73}$ $\overline{17}$ $\overline{80}$ $\overline{37}$ $\overline{85}$ $\overline{101}$
Start of the US Constitution

$\overline{76}$ $\overline{105}$ $\overline{59}$ $\overline{11}$ $\overline{70}$ $\overline{51}$ $\overline{15}$ $\overline{26}$
Gold, silver, and iron (but not bronze)

$\overline{90}$ $\overline{19}$ $\overline{13}$ $\overline{20}$ $\overline{97}$ $\overline{69}$ $\overline{71}$ $\overline{55}$ $\overline{61}$ $\overline{23}$
Email add-on

$\overline{95}$ $\overline{109}$ $\overline{46}$ $\overline{100}$ $\overline{103}$ $\overline{2}$
_____ burner (lab device)

$\overline{91}$ $\overline{99}$ $\overline{41}$ $\overline{30}$ $\overline{22}$ $\overline{106}$
Beat the shit out of

ELIZABETH WURTZEL

Replacement parts are unavailable in *Prozac Nation*.

1		2	3	4	5		6	7	8	9		10		11
12	13	14		15	16	17		18	19	20		21	22	23
24	25	26	27	28		29	30	31	32		33	34	35	36
	37	38	39		40	41	42	43	44	45		46	47	48
	49	50		51	52	53	54	55	56	57		58	59	60
61	62	63		64	65	66	67		68	69	70	71	72	
73	74		75	76	77	78		79	80	81		82	83	84
85	86	87	88		89	90	91	92	93	94		95	96	97
	98	99	100	101	102	103	104	105		106	107	108		109
110	111													

5 86 49 90 100 30 42 8
Famously dirty type of poem

72 76 55 56 61 77 43 20 95
Place-name often featured in the above

50 67 88 68 4 53 48 85 105
Tomorrow, two days from now

2 87 107 108 11 7 57 91 60 101 63
_____ Coppola (director of The Godfather)

27 32 98 10 103 22 78 28
Owner of the infamous "blue dress"

19 109 16 17 25 99 31
Dustin, Abbie, or Philip Seymour

102 6 46 23 70 65
Largest US state

66 71 81 13 80 47 104
State that's home to Ben and Jerry's ice cream

21 62 12 26 52 73 69
Montgomery is this state's capital

45 54 9 51 58 15 38 18 59
General geographic location of the above

24 1 33 40 83 29
Famous Parisian tower

106 35 36 64 44 82
Newsman Dan

89 74 94 84 3 93
Cell phone predecessor big in the 1980s

92 41 39 37 79 111 96 97 75 34 110 14
Like a shot _____ (unexpected event descriptor)

FRENCH INSULT

Write the word that answers all three clues. Then black out each letter in this answer in the random list of letters on the next page. What remains is an English translation of the French insult *Je te pisse à la raie!*

1. _____ and hawed

2. _____ in (surrounded)

3. Adjusted one's pant legs, maybe

_ _ _ _ _

HDIHPIDS

HSEEOHND

YODUEREB

MUHTHTMC

DREAECHK

LOOK AROUND

Or maybe you're one of them?

$\overline{44}$ $\overline{27}$ $\overline{42}$ $\overline{108}$ $\overline{37}$ $\overline{103}$ $\overline{54}$ $\overline{13}$ $\overline{11}$ $\overline{101}$ $\overline{104}$ $\overline{40}$ $\overline{78}$
Author of the quote

$\overline{26}$ $\overline{29}$ $\overline{77}$ $\overline{97}$ $\overline{69}$ $\overline{84}$ $\overline{94}$ $\overline{66}$ $\overline{18}$ $\overline{60}$ $\overline{23}$ $\overline{90}$ $\overline{16}$ $\overline{12}$ $\overline{24}$ $\overline{47}$ $\overline{102}$
1989 rom-com with Billy Crystal and Meg Ryan

$\overline{41}$ $\overline{52}$ $\overline{59}$ $\overline{88}$ $\overline{5}$ $\overline{39}$ $\overline{95}$ $\overline{55}$ $\overline{71}$ $\overline{106}$ $\overline{46}$ $\overline{87}$ $\overline{109}$ $\overline{98}$ $\overline{56}$
1983 Star Wars release, with "The"

$\overline{73}$ $\overline{62}$ $\overline{86}$ $\overline{8}$ $\overline{1}$ $\overline{67}$ $\overline{21}$ $\overline{25}$ $\overline{49}$ $\overline{105}$ $\overline{28}$
German festival held every September (ironically)

$\overline{36}$ $\overline{32}$ $\overline{19}$ $\overline{20}$ $\overline{110}$ $\overline{34}$ $\overline{45}$
Husbands and wives

$\overline{70}$ $\overline{14}$ $\overline{75}$ $\overline{85}$ $\overline{4}$ $\overline{82}$ $\overline{100}$ $\overline{61}$
"My _____ don't want none unless you got buns, hun!"

$\overline{107}$ $\overline{10}$ $\overline{7}$ $\overline{22}$ $\overline{58}$ $\overline{31}$ $\overline{96}$ $\overline{64}$
Ancient Greek epic hero

$\overline{3}$ $\overline{74}$ $\overline{68}$ $\overline{65}$ $\overline{33}$ $\overline{6}$
Back to the _____ (1985 sci-fi classic)

$\overline{50}$ $\overline{92}$ $\overline{57}$ $\overline{17}$ $\overline{48}$ $\overline{79}$ $\overline{43}$ $\overline{51}$ $\overline{99}$ $\overline{30}$
Like a mountain goat, say

$\overline{83}$ $\overline{15}$ $\overline{9}$ $\overline{93}$ $\overline{2}$ $\overline{72}$ $\overline{63}$ $\overline{89}$
Bully's insult toward the bespectacled

$\overline{91}$ $\overline{80}$ $\overline{38}$ $\overline{76}$ $\overline{81}$ $\overline{53}$ $\overline{35}$
Skyscraper count

KEEP IT PG

Use these for the moments in mixed company.

5 LETTERS
Frack

Sugar

6 LETTERS
Phooey

Shucks

7 LETTERS
Criminy

Jeepers

Shitake

8 LETTERS
Bull Spit

Holy Heck

9 LETTERS
Son of a Gun

11 LETTERS
Judas Priest

12 LETTERS
Fudge Nuggets

ALLITERATIVE ALLURE

Don't be a ding-dong about this puzzle.

8 LETTERS
Fuckface

9 LETTERS
Shitstain

Tatertits

10 LETTERS
Buttbatter

Cockchafer

Dickdipper

Nadnibbler

11 LETTERS
Goochgoblin

Horsehumper

FILTHY PHILIAS

How well do you know deviant sexual fetishes? Draw a line from each fetish to its correct sexual obsession.

Acrotomophilia	Getting mugged
Gerontophilia	Obscene words
Chremastistophilia	Piercings/tattoos
Dacryphilia	Armpits
Eproctophilia	The elderly
Formicophilia	Urination
Hybristophilia	Hair
Maschalagnia	Criminals
Narratophilia	Flatulence
Stigmatophilia	Amputees
Trichophilia	People crying
Urolagnia	Crawling insects

ICELANDIC INSULT

Write the word that answers all three clues. Then black out each letter in this answer in the random list of letters on the next page. What remains is an English translation of the Icelandic insult *Hoppaðu upp í rassgatið á þér!*

1. Dick, in other words
2. Part of an HBO crime drama title
3. Spade or Poirot

_ _ _ _ _ _ _ _ _

EHDOPUI

CIPYTDE

OUIRTDC

OCTDWIN

DAVESIS

BOOB EUPHEMISMS

Can you decode these euphemisms for female breasts?
Every phrase uses the same substitution cipher.
We've given you the first one to help you get started.
(For example: E becomes H; M becomes B; etc.)

HIGH BEAMS
EDWE MRHJZ

_____ _____
BUHPPDX ZBNYYRUZ

_____ _____
ZLRHBRU ZBURBXERUZ

_____ _____
PUNOBHI INMRZ

_____ _____
PUNZB KRBRXBNUZ

_____ _____
QNWWDOW YHUBORUZ

_____ _____
MNMMZRF BLDOZ

_____ _____
XNOWN MNOWNZ

_____ _____
WRUMRU ZRUCRUZ

_____ _____
ZDHJRZR BLDOZ

ZENTIKRU MNTIKRUZ

QDWWIR MHWZ

JRHB JNTOBHDOZ

JNOSRF MTJYZ

BETOKRU QTWZ

KNTMIR MTMMIRZ

ZEDUB BTUODYZ

MNNMDX JNTOKZ

JDIS JDZZDIRZ

YHUBF YROKTITJZ

DAN CARR

Don't let the bastards get you down!

<u>77</u> <u>22</u> <u>4</u> <u>18</u> <u>113</u> <u>11</u> <u>90</u> <u>75</u> <u>19</u> <u>81</u> <u>59</u> <u>103</u> <u>60</u> <u>110</u> <u>3</u> <u>26</u>

Southern comedian with the line: "Get 'er done!"

<u>72</u> <u>28</u> <u>115</u> <u>114</u> <u>101</u> <u>95</u> <u>1</u> <u>42</u> <u>10</u> <u>96</u> <u>32</u> <u>84</u> <u>8</u> <u>53</u> <u>35</u>

YOLO

<u>93</u> <u>88</u> <u>15</u> <u>64</u> <u>13</u> <u>69</u> <u>24</u> <u>82</u> <u>83</u>

Chute sport

<u>102</u> <u>107</u> <u>94</u> <u>41</u> <u>29</u> <u>30</u> <u>14</u> <u>112</u> <u>2</u> <u>92</u> <u>34</u> <u>97</u> <u>66</u> <u>20</u> <u>80</u> <u>108</u>

Star Wars movie that introduced Jar Jar Binks

<u>58</u> <u>74</u> <u>70</u> <u>21</u> <u>7</u> <u>76</u> <u>23</u> <u>56</u>

Bikini alternative

<u>6</u> <u>63</u> <u>40</u> <u>47</u> <u>44</u> <u>43</u> <u>85</u> <u>27</u> <u>111</u> <u>38</u> <u>48</u>

Twelve quarters, ten dimes, and three nickels

<u>52</u> <u>61</u> <u>62</u> <u>105</u> <u>54</u> <u>98</u> <u>50</u>

Self-centered sort

<u>109</u> <u>45</u> <u>106</u> <u>73</u> <u>46</u>

Hashtag sexual harassment movement

<u>33</u> <u>71</u> <u>79</u> <u>65</u> <u>87</u> <u>16</u> <u>67</u> <u>104</u> <u>37</u>

910 and 912 but definitely not 911

<u>51</u> <u>91</u> <u>31</u> <u>100</u> <u>89</u> <u>9</u> <u>39</u> <u>57</u> <u>49</u>

"Hopelessly _____ You" (Olivia Newton-John song of 1978)

<u>12</u> <u>17</u> <u>68</u> <u>55</u> <u>5</u>

"Blue ____ Shoes" (Elvis song of 1956)

<u>36</u> <u>25</u> <u>86</u> <u>99</u> <u>78</u>

Sexy men

DUTCH INSULT

Write the letters that complete this puzzle. (Hint: There's a president missing.) Then black out each letter in this answer in the random list of letters on the next page. What remains is an English translation of the Dutch insult *Ik laat een scheet in jouw richting!*

RWR GHWB WJC _ _ _ BHO DJT

REVISED EDITION Now with "Fuck"!

Although a commonly used word since the early Renaissance, "fuck" didn't appear in a single English-language dictionary between 1795 and 1965. It reappeared in *The Penguin Dictionary* in 1966.

I F G A B R W

T I G N B Y G

O U R G D B I

B R E W C B T

G I O G N W B

ANTHONY LICCIONE

Which category do you fit in?

1	2	3	4	5		6	7	8		9	10	11	12	
13	14	15	16	17		18	19		20	21	22	23	24	25
	26	27		28	29	30	31	32		33	34		35	36
37		38	39	40	41	42			43	44	45		46	47
48	49	50	51	52	53		54	55	56		57	58	59
60	61	62	63	64		65	66	67		68	69	70	
71	72	73	74	75	76	77		78	79	80		81	82
83	84	85		86	87	88	89		90	91	92	93		94
95	96	97		98	99	100	101		102	103	104		105	106
107	108		109	110	111								

<u>93</u> <u>55</u> <u>3</u> <u>38</u> <u>105</u> <u>51</u> <u>9</u> <u>27</u> <u>19</u> <u>94</u> <u>88</u> <u>96</u> <u>24</u> <u>74</u> <u>43</u> <u>40</u> <u>5</u> <u>52</u> <u>86</u>
Scorcese/DiCaprio film set in New York (2013)

<u>17</u> <u>44</u> <u>111</u> <u>54</u> <u>81</u> <u>37</u> <u>7</u> <u>31</u> <u>59</u> <u>97</u> <u>57</u> <u>79</u> <u>42</u>
Scorcese/DiCaprio film set in an asylum (2010)

<u>65</u> <u>36</u> <u>45</u> <u>80</u> <u>21</u> <u>23</u> <u>68</u> <u>4</u> <u>1</u> <u>8</u> <u>32</u>
Scorcese/DiCaprio film set in Boston (2006)

<u>26</u> <u>82</u> <u>25</u> <u>102</u> <u>29</u> <u>72</u> <u>78</u> <u>35</u> <u>18</u> <u>108</u>
Scorcese/DiCaprio film about Howard Hughes (2004)

<u>90</u> <u>22</u> <u>2</u> <u>15</u> <u>60</u> <u>61</u> <u>103</u> <u>13</u> <u>63</u> <u>48</u>
_____ Booth (infamous assassin)

<u>20</u> <u>83</u> <u>41</u> <u>71</u> <u>28</u>
Polish dance

<u>106</u> <u>11</u> <u>14</u> <u>89</u> <u>101</u> <u>110</u> <u>34</u>
Louis _____ (luxury brand)

<u>99</u> <u>10</u> <u>76</u> <u>70</u> <u>75</u> <u>64</u> <u>66</u> <u>50</u> <u>107</u> <u>69</u>
"Close only counts in _____ and hand grenades."

<u>62</u> <u>91</u> <u>92</u> <u>77</u> <u>109</u>
Word with cat or hound

<u>46</u> <u>104</u> <u>33</u> <u>6</u> <u>84</u> <u>67</u> <u>53</u>
Pseudonyms listed on a wanted poster

<u>16</u> <u>95</u> <u>47</u> <u>49</u> <u>85</u> <u>58</u>
Real beauties, in slang

<u>87</u> <u>30</u> <u>39</u> <u>98</u> <u>100</u> <u>56</u> <u>12</u> <u>73</u>
Nickname for Indiana natives

FINISH THAT QUOTE

We've given you six famous (and filthy) partial movie quotes and a list of words. Use each word to complete all six quotes, you filthy animal!

You need a license to buy a dog or drive a car. Hell, you need a license to catch a fish. But they'll let any _butt_ -_reaming asshole be a father_

— Tod Higgins, *Parenthood*

The only reason I did this is because you're my nephew and I love you. If it were anybody else, they would've gotten that intervention _through the back of their fucking head_

— Tony Soprano, *The Sopranos*

I bet you're the kind of guy that would fuck a person in the ass and not even have the goddamn common courtesy to _give him a reach -around_.

— Gunnery Sgt. Hartman, *Full Metal Jacket*

WORD BANK

~~a~~	~~asshole~~	~~butt~~	~~father~~	~~get~~
~~a~~	~~back~~	~~choose~~	~~fucking~~	~~give~~
~~around~~	~~be~~	~~every~~	~~fucking~~	~~head~~

Let me tell you something: There's no nobility in poverty. I've been a rich man and I've been a poor man. And I _choose_ **rich every fucking time.**

— Jordan Belfort, *The Wolf of Wall Street*

Now when you yell at me, it makes me nervous. And when I get nervous, I get scared. And when **motherfuckers get scared**, that's when motherfuckers accidentally get shot.

— Jules Winnfield, *Pulp Fiction*

Wish in one hand and **shit in the other** one. See which one fills up first.

— Willie T. Soke, *Bad Santa*

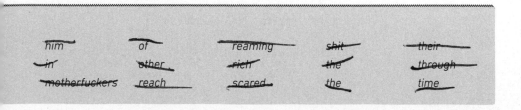

~~him~~   ~~of~~   ~~reaming~~   ~~shit~~   ~~their~~
~~in~~   ~~other~~   ~~rich~~   ~~the~~   ~~through~~
~~motherfuckers~~   reach   ~~scared~~   the   time

CHUCK PALAHNIUK
You too can make others jealous.

‾‾‾‾‾‾‾ ‾‾‾‾‾‾ ‾‾‾‾‾‾ ‾‾‾‾‾‾
GJPKVGR CWVMTY FTJFUT LWBEVTW

‾‾‾‾ ‾‾‾‾‾‾ ‾‾‾‾‾‾‾ ‾‾‾‾
PKBG YTTVGR YJATJGT KBMT

‾ ‾‾‾‾ ‾‾‾‾‾‾‾‾ ‾‾‾‾.
B RJJC QZLOVGR UVQT.

BOB HUGHES
This *Drugstore Cowboy* can help you find your purpose.

‾‾‾‾‾'‾ ‾‾‾‾‾‾‾ ‾‾‾‾
WFRCR'T LHWFKLV IHCR

‾‾‾‾-‾‾‾‾‾‾‾‾ ‾‾‾‾
MKOR-UOOKCIKLV WFUL

‾‾‾‾‾‾‾ ‾‾‾ ‾‾‾‾
VRWWKLV WFR TFKW

‾‾‾‾‾‾ ‾‾‾ ‾‾ ‾‾‾.
NKDNRP HAW HO QHA.

CROATIAN INSULT

Use the provided key to decode the English-language translation of this Croatian insult: *Idi u pičku materinu!*

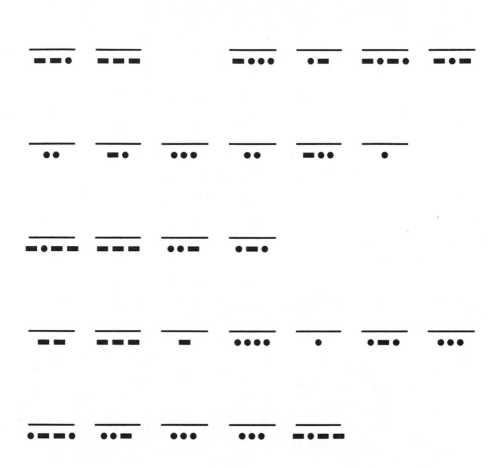

A	B	C	D	E	F	G	H	I	J	K	L	M
·—	—···	—·—·	—··	·	··—·	——·	····	··	·———	—·—	·—··	——

N	O	P	Q	R	S	T	U	V	W	X	Y	Z
—·	———	·——·	——·—	·—·	···	—	··—	···—	·——	—··—	—·——	——··

FRENCH CURSES

As my French teacher used to say,
"Ah ah ah, en français!" Not only do you need
to find the French words, but you also need
to find their English translations.

```
B K Z N P K A Q T Q K
D R A N N O C U Q C T
C E V H C T I B O A N
P P B S H I T N B S I
L O R E T W N G R S A
J L A O H A A B T H T
G A N P S Z E N T O U
F S L S T T T U K L P
U G E Z C V E D R E M
C C U N T L Q W I N R
K P R D M O U U F H M
```

Asshole   Connasse   Putain
Bitch   Cunt   Salope
Branleur   Fuck   Shit
Connard   Merde   Wanker

SEVEN-LETTER WORDS

We've hidden 24 different insulting and/or impolite 7-letter words in this puzzle. How many can you find?

```
T I T T I E S S A B M U D
U J A C K A S S F A C E A
N G T N A S S I P I U L W
K N N B N G O D D A M N K
C F H G A B K C I D A B C
U D A B M A X N U I P A I
F O N K A S S W I P E S D
B U K K A K E S A S S S R
F C C X X K F U B H H H A
X H T I H S T A B I I O T
S E I B O O B A V T T L S
N Y C O C K W A D A D E A
S C U M B A G A B L L A B
```

YIDDISH INSULT

Write the word that answers all three clues. Then black out each letter in this answer in the random list of letters on the next page. What remains is an English translation of the Yiddish insult
Gay kocken offen yom!

1. Prepare a male porn star
2. Pillow action
3. _____ piece (inconsequential story)

_ _ _ _ _

UGLOSU

HLILTU

IUNLTL

HFEUOU

CFEALN

FIVE-LETTER WORDS

We've hidden 23 different insulting and/or impolite
5-letter words in this puzzle. How many can you find?

```
R T T N F B W P U S S Y
Y H S U T K P D E K Y G K
H C T I B C P C Q N W N A
E A R S T I M H O U I V N
F V I R H R A J K O E S K
B L W B E P R B Y B Z E H
P U Y H R N T R T O W E F
O V V U O L O A O I C N F
R T G O E R C B O N Y U D
N Q A D B O E U B K G I D
O C O I O M X F Y L L I W
A H C C N D I K Y D E E V
C E H N S T T B O J I Q O
```

_____ _____ _____

_____ _____ _____

_____ _____ _____

_____ _____ _____

_____ _____ _____

_____ _____ _____

EIGHT-LETTER WORDS

We've hidden 19 different insulting and/or impolite
8-letter words in this puzzle. How many can you find?

```
N W T S R E K C O N K O S
D E E W K C I D Q C I D V
O T S H Q G E N A T T B R
J S T Y A E O S A G X U O
Q E I J W W T L C N K N T
H F C L L I L R P A C G A
A T L A H E E W L T A H R
R I E S F A M J V N S O B
D H A C M K A A T O L L I
C S L P D I C K H O L E V
O N I K S E R O F P A I R
R E A S S M U N C H B K P
E S P U N K W A D Y S Y K
```

_____   _____   _____

_____   _____   _____

_____   _____   _____

_____   _____   _____

_____   _____   _____

              _____

PENN JILLETTE

It's almost like magic.

```
_____ , _ _____ _____ . . .
HMYJY'T KXHMFKN RYHHYJ . . .
__ ___ _____ ____ _____ _____ ____
FK HMY UXJQL HMEK TXDYXKY UMXTY QFCY
___ _____ __ ___ __ _ _____
UET CBAIYL BG EKL PXB LX E QFHHQY
_____ ___ ___ _____ ____ ___ , _ .
TXDYHMFKN EKL KXU HMYFJ QFCY FTK'H.
```

GORDON RAMSAY

We didn't forget this famous chef who enjoys cursing.

```
___ ' __ ___ _____ _____ __ __
XUF'JH RUA HJHEX EYRMA AU CH
_____ _____ ___ _____ __ .
VDYRMADX ZFNGHP UZZ SCUFA YA.
_____ _ _____ __ __ _
CHNSFVH Y BUFDP CH YZ Y
_____ ____ ____ .
NUUGHP AMSA VMYA.
```

COURTNEY LOVE
It's all about purpose.

```
__ _ _____,' ___ _____
QP Q PIFMQV' EQT XQOYCIO

_____ _____ ___,' _____,
YHBQVA XWQOOTV OXC, OYWTT,

__ ____ _____ ____ _____ ...
CW PCIW ZWQDDQHVO WCFM LCVAL ...

_ ___,_ ____ ___ _ _____ __ ____.
Q ECV'O MVCX XYK Q DQBTE SK DQPT.
```

FRANK ZAPPA
When people show their true selves, believe them.

```
_____ ___ _____ _____.
WRSWYR GUR VGBDQGYYC BKDXXC.

__,_ ____ ____ _____ __ ____
DX'B TKRE XKRC WUSZR DX SZRU

___ ____ _____ ____ __
GEA SZRU GNGDE XKGX DX

____ _____.
NRXB SVESMDSJB.
```

ROMANIAN INSULT

Use the provided key to decode the English-language translation of this Romanian insult:

Uscamias chilotii pe crucea matii!

A	B	C	D	E	F	G	H	I	J	K	L	M
.-	-...	-.-.	-..	.	..-.	--.	....	..	.---	-.-	.-..	--

N	O	P	Q	R	S	T	U	V	W	X	Y	Z
-.	---	.--.	--.-	.-.	...	-	..-	...-	.--	-..-	-.--	--..

SURROUNDED BY ASSHOLES

To escape, use the letters **A**, **S**, **S**, **H**, **O**, **L**, and **E** once each for each puzzle to complete these terms.

G_____
(Rainy-day footwear)

C___E ___V_
(Nerve-racking narrow escape)

_B__I____
(Eradicates)

H_T F_____
(Menopausal symptoms)

___E__C__
(Sneaker securers)

___L__W__T
(Least deep)

F_____O_D_
(Lies)

K____R ___T
(Large-crystaled cooking ingredient)

__I__T_N__
(Frozen precipitation pellets)

B___P__M_U_
(Disrespectful, religion-wise)

_I_N'_ ___R_
(Biggest portion)

STEPHEN KING

Perspective is everything with this guy.

```
_____ ___ _____ ____ __ _____,
EDIABWQS XZQ HSQYX JYRR DO EZBIY,

__ ___ ____: ___ _____ __ _ ____, ___.
BO CDV JBRR: DIQ AXDIQ YX Y XBNQ, NYI.

____ _ ___. ___ _____ __ _ ____.
XZYX'A YRR. DIQ AXDIQ YX Y XBNQ.

___ _'__ ____ ___ ___ ___ ____
FVX B'MQ SQYW CDV EYI AQQ XZYX

_____ ____ _____
NDXZQSOVEPQS OSDN ATYEQ

_____ _ _____.
JBXZDVX Y XQRQAEDTQ.
```

HARLAN ELLISON

Did he really go there?

```
_ _____ ____ __ _ _____ _____,
G MWGII JLAD LQ V BVQFVI WNYZJAGWZA,

__ _____, ___ __ _____ ___
RN HELGHZ, VQT WL WELMZ JEL

_____ __ _ _____, _ ___:
HLQMGTZA BZ V IFTTGWZ, G MVN:

"____ ___ ___ __ ____."
"UFHD NLF VQT NL BVBV."
```

AMY WINEHOUSE
She sure as hell didn't!

‾‾ , ‾‾‾ ‾‾‾‾‾‾‾‾ ‾‾ ‾‾ ‾‾
OE'U WKE OHXKYECWE EK HG EK

‾‾‾‾ ‾‾‾‾‾ ‾‾‾‾‾‾ ‾‾ ‾‾‾‾ .
HCLG KEJGY XGKXPG CE GCUG.

‾ ‾‾ ‾‾‾‾‾‾‾‾‾‾ , ‾‾‾ ‾‾‾‾ , ‾
O CH ZOQQOSI⌐C, RIE EJCE'U

‾ ‾‾‾‾‾ ‾ ‾‾‾ , ‾ ‾‾‾‾‾‾ ‾‾‾‾ ‾ ‾‾‾‾ .
'SCIUG O ZKW'E YGCPPF VONG C QISL.

MITCH HEDBERG
You're surrounded by the needed materials.

‾‾ ‾‾‾ ‾‾‾‾ ‾‾‾‾‾‾‾‾ ‾‾‾‾ ‾‾ ‾‾‾
MC LWZ CMDK LWZOTREC EWTQ MD QJR

‾‾‾‾‾ , ‾‾‾‾ ‾‾ , ‾‾‾‾‾ ‾ ‾‾‾‾‾ .
PWWKT, CZGY MQ, SZMEK I JWZTR.

SPANISH CURSES

I was my Spanish teacher's favorite student.
He would always say to me: "*¡Idiota! ¡En español!*"
Not only do you need to find the Spanish words,
but you also need to find their English translations.

```
I D I O T A M V R K X
I H K C P I Y S C T N
S J O D E R Q U T A O
S Y H R N N F T O R R
A M D S D R A T S A B
B A H N E J P I R D A
M R P B J A T U P O C
U I W H O R E M S Q X
D C Y N O R O M Y S D
V O T I H S L L U B Y
D N Y T E L O H S S A
```

Asshole	Idiota	Pussy
Bastard	Joder	Puta
Bullshit	Maricón	Tarado
Cabrón	Mierda	Whore
Dumbass	Moron	
Fuck	Pendejo	

SIX-LETTER WORDS

We've hidden 25 different insulting and/or impolite 6-letter words in this puzzle. How many can you find?

```
E  S  S  B  X  Y  P  P  A  R  C  N  W
O  H  P  E  T  S  U  T  A  H  S  S  A
C  I  O  A  Z  S  K  A  K  H  A  N  N
F  T  O  V  K  B  C  T  M  R  I  Y  K
U  T  G  E  G  E  U  L  G  G  F  P  E
C  Y  E  R  I  C  F  F  A  F  E  R  R
K  Z  K  K  H  U  F  V  I  C  R  M  E
E  O  O  U  X  O  W  T  K  L  E  E  S
R  O  S  A  G  I  S  E  H  I  T  M  S
D  L  L  A  E  N  R  G  F  M  O  B  I
K  F  J  N  E  N  V  X  M  A  O  E  P
E  T  E  S  T  E  S  N  S  X  C  R  M
C  R  O  T  C  H  L  A  S  S  B  A  G
```

_____	_____	_____
_____	_____	_____
_____	_____	_____
_____	_____	_____
_____	_____	_____
_____	_____	_____
_____	_____	
_____	_____	

BILLY CORGAN

He's still smashing conventions.

```
_ ___'_ _____ _____ ____
P UTG'F GLOLKKQJPMD HLMPLAL FIQF

___ _____ __ _____ __ _
FIL KFPGW TE EQPMCJL PK Q

___ _____. __ _____ ___
HQU FIPGW. PF WPALK DTC

_ _____ _____ __ _____
Q OLJFQPG QYTCGF TE EJLLUTY

__ ____ ___ ____ __!
FT BCKF KQD ECOS PF!
```

TOM ROBBINS

That's one way to calculate each word you write.

```
_'__ _____ _____ _____ _____
Q'GG RDHDL ILQZD MRVZYDL RVHDG

__ __ _____ _____.
VR MR DGDPZLQP ZTEDILQZDL.

_'_ _____ ___ _ ____ ____
Q'F LMZYDL WKD M KYMLE KZQPC

___ _ _____ ____ __ ___ ____.
MRF M GQZZGD EQGD VJ FVA KYQZ.
```

KEN KESEY

Don't let that cuckoo idea take you over.

```
___ ___ __ ___ _____ __ __
ZOY RKL KA ZOY TWDZYW DJ ZK

____ __ ___,  __ _____ ___
NDJJ PK MJJ,  PK FMZZYW OKT

___ ___ ____ ___ _____
LDU MPS OKVB MPS TODZY

___ _____ ___ _____.
MPS ZYFXZDPU MPS XKTYWACV.
```

GEORGE CARLIN

What a scary thought!

```
____ _____ __ ____ __ _____
LKJM SCZDLOE JM YZII CY DJLPJLM

___ _____. ___ ____ _____ ____?
HDR HMMKCIGM. ECZ GFGO DCLJSG LKHL?

_____, _____, _____, _____,
DJLPJLM, HMMKCIGM, YZSWZNM, MSZTQHVM,

_____, ___ _____.
XGOWCYYM, HDR RJNMKJLM.

___ ____ ___ ____.
HDR LKGE HII FCLG.
```

THE F*CK ANSW

KING
VERS

16 FIND THE FUCK

```
C K F F U C F U C U U F F U U
F F F C F C F C U F U F F C F
C F K U C U K F K C C C C F F
C K K F K C K K U U K U C F C
K C C U F C U F U F C F C F C
U F C U K U U U F C F U C C K
U K U F U F C K F U F C K C F
U K K F F F U U F F U F F F K
F U U U F K U F C C F K C U U
U C U K F U U U K U C C C F U
U F C C U U K U K U C K F U C
K F U K C F F U F F U C C K U
U K C C F K U C U F C F K K F
F U K F F C K C K U F K F F C
U U C U U F C K C C K C C F K
K K C F U K C K U U U U F F U
U U F U U K U K U K K C U C C
K K K K C U K C K K F U U K C
```

17 SOLVE THIS FUCKING PUZZLE OR ...

```
P . . . . E A T S H I T
I . . . . . A . . . . O
S U C K A D I C K . . U
S . . . . . E . . . . G
O . K I S S M Y A S S H
F . . . H . . H . . . S
F U C K Y O U . I . . H
. P . . V . . K . . . I
. Y . . G E T B E N T T
. O . . I . . . . . .
. U . G E T F U C K E D
. R . . . . . . . . .
. S U C K A S S . . .
```

18 FIVE-FINGER SHUFFLE

Tug the slug
Spank the monkey
Beat the meat
Wax the carrot
Choke the chicken
Bash the bishop
Jerkin' the gherkin
Pull the pork

Flog the dog
Strangle the snake
Slap the salami
Jack the beanstalk

19 DICKING AROUND

Pecker
Member
Pickle
Salami
Johnson
Sausage
Manhood
Package

20 VERY EASY WORD ARITHMETIC

2=G, 3=B, 4=S, 7=A

20 REBUS EXCLAMATION

what in the fuck

21 DILLWEED & FUCKFACE

	DILL
Boys ____ be boys	WILL
Word with oil or wishing	WELL
Metalworker's job	WELD
	WEED
	FUCK
Shit out of ____	LUCK
Be deficient in	LACK
Lingerie material	LACE
	FACE

22 DOUBLE-BARRELED NONOGRAM

Row clues:
6
2, 2, 2
1, 2, 1
8
1, 5, 2, 1
1, 3, 3, 1
1, 6, 1
3, 2, 3
4, 2, 4
10
6
2
2
4
2, 2
2, 2
2, 2
2, 2
3, 3
3, 3

23 MARILYN MANSON

Most of the world's problems could be avoided if people just said what they fucking meant.

23 BARNYARD PICTOGRAM

ass over teakettle

24 OBSCENE TELEPHONE

UPYOURS
GETBENT
ASSHOLE
BASTARD
DICKWAD
FUCKWIT
SHITBAG
DUMBASS
SCHMUCK

25 URGENT PICTOGRAM

cut the crap

25 GILLIAN ANDERSON

When I think of normalcy, I think of mediocrity—and mediocrity scares the fuck out of me.

26 NONOGRAM ADVICE

Row clues:
3, 1, 1, 3, 1, 1
1, 1, 1, 1, 1, 1
3, 1, 1, 1, 2
1, 1, 1, 1, 1, 1
1, 3, 3, 1, 1
0
1, 1, 3, 1, 1, 3
1, 1, 1, 1, 1, 1, 1, 1
3, 1, 1, 1, 3
1, 1, 1, 1, 1, 2
1, 3, 3, 1, 1
0
3, 3, 1, 3
1, 1, 1, 1
3, 2, 1, 3
1, 1, 1, 1
3, 3, 3, 1

27 FOODIE PICTOGRAM

shit sandwich

27 JEN FAULKNER

When people say "There are other fish in the sea," I say: "Fuck you, she was my sea."

28 PROFANITY PROFICIENCY

Beard-Splitter (a) A person who regularly visits prostitutes

You can imagine what the "beard" in this term might represent! As an insult, "beard-splitter" dates at least back to the early 18th century.

(Later, it would morph into a generalized term for a man's penis.)

Roiderbanks (c) One who spends beyond their means

Presumably, this word originated from calling someone who was an inveterate spender a "bank raider."

Abydocomist (b) One who lies often and is proud of it

Abydos was an ancient town in what is now modern-day Turkey whose inhabitants were said to have been inveterate liars and slanderers who actively boasted of their inventions.

Scobberlotcher (a) An idle, lazy person

This term dates back at least to the 1600s and might derive from the Old English word scopperloit, which meant "to loiter."

Smellfungus (d) A fault-finding buzzkill

"Smellfungus" was originally the name of a character in Laurence Sterne's 1768 novel *A Sentimental Journey Through France and Italy*. No matter what he saw in his travels, he always found a way to find fault in it and describe it in an overly negative light. By the early 1800s, the term was widely used to describe any hypernegative complainer.

Rakefire (b) A guest who overstays their welcome

For most of history, it was common practice to entertain guests around the hearth or fireplace, and when the fire was down to just smoldering embers, that was an unspoken hint that it was time for the guest to leave. Not for this guy though! He'd literally "rake the fire" to keep the embers going so he could stay longer, thus overstaying his welcome.

Rantallion (c) A guy with a small dick.

A 1788 book called *The Dictionary of the Vulgar Tongue* defined a rantallion as someone "whose shot pouch is longer than the barrel of his piece." In other words, his scrotum is longer than his penis. Some argue this could be used as a compliment, such as "He has huge balls!" But most agree: It just means he's got a teensy-weensy dick.

Bobolyne (c) A stupid fool.

This term was first written down by John Skelton (tutor to King Henry VIII, of wife-killing fame) in the early 1500s. No one is quite sure of the etymology though!

Snoutband (a) A know-it-all who constantly interrupts other people

Everyone knows the guy who constantly interrupts the conversation with "Well actually ..." Presumably, he interrupts so frequently that you want to "band his snout" (that is, shut him the fuck up!).

Skelpie-limmer (b) A rambunctious, naughty young girl

This Scottish term combines "skelp" (meaning to smack with an open hand) and "limmer" (meaning a roguish, promiscuous woman). It was generally only used against young girls to warn them of the pitfalls of bad behavior.

---

30   NEAL STEPHENSON

Until a man is twenty-five, he still thinks every so often that under the right circumstances, he could be the baddest motherfucker in the world.

KINGOFTHEWORLD NEWYORKCITY LEONARDODAVINCI MACHIAVELLI STRETCHER SLUSHFUND FISHNET THETRUTH BITESTHEDUST EATME BUTCHER TENEMENTS

---

32   WHO GIVES A FUCK?

Fruitcake
Fullback
Unfrock
Cufflink
Fire truck
Chock full
Jackfruit
Huck Finn
Daffy Duck

33 WHO GIVES A SHIT?

Shift
Shoplift
Shipment
Masochist
Schnitzel
Gesundheit
Syphilitic
Flashlight
Psychologist
Sophisticated

34 MITCH HEDBERG

They say Flintstones vitamins are chewable. All vitamins are chewable, it's just that they taste shitty.

34 RUST COHLE

If the only thing keeping a person decent is the expectation of divine reward, then, brother, that person is a piece of shit.

35 EASY WORD ARITHMETIC

0=T, 4=U, 5=S, 6=N, 7=A, 8=B

0=U, 1=T, 3=S, 4=Y, 5=I, 6=P, 8=H

0=L, 1=O, 2=E, 3=F, 4=N, 5=R, 6=I, 7=D, 8=G, 9=M

36 MEDIUM WORD ARITHMETIC

0=I, 1=A, 2=D, 3=B, 4=H, 5=M, 6=T, 7=S, 8=C

0=I, 1=W, 2=R, 3=U, 4=C, 5=E, 6=S, 7=D, 8=K, 9=A

1=C, 2=I, 3=T, 4=S, 5=A, 6=H, 7=Y, 8=B

37 WORDOKU

K	A	E	W	N	R
N	W	R	A	K	E
A	R	K	N	E	W
W	E	N	K	R	A
R	N	W	E	A	K
E	K	A	R	W	N

37 WORDOKU

U	N	G	S	D	I
I	S	D	U	G	N
N	G	I	D	S	U
S	D	U	N	I	G
D	I	N	G	U	S
G	U	S	I	N	D

38 MEDIUM WORD ARITHMETIC

0=A, 1=D, 2=G, 3=O, 4=B, 5=I, 6=C, 7=K, 8=S, 9=F

39 BALLS DEEP

40 SPANISH INSULTS

I hope you get fucked by a fish! (*¡Que te folle un pez!*)

I shit in the milk! (*¡Me cago en la leche!*)

I shit in the whore that gave birth to you! (*¡Me cago en la puta que te parió!*)

The parrot's pussy! (*¡La concha de la lora!*)

41 LOUIS CK

Eat a big bag of dicks

42 ASSHOLE & BULLSHIT

	ASS
Girl, in Scotland	LASS
At a ____ for words	LOSS
Misplace	LOSE
Shoe part	SOLE
	HOLE

	BULL
Bird's beak	BILL
Window feature	SILL
River deposit	SILT
Slang for vagina	SLIT
	SHIT

43 GEN. JAMES "MAD DOG" MATTIS

I come in peace. I didn't bring artillery. But I'm pleading with you, with tears in my eyes: If you fuck with me, I'll kill you all.

43 OZZY FUCKING OSBOURNE

I'm not picking up dog shit. I'm a rock star.

44 BUTTHOLE & CRAPHOLE

	BUTT
Woman's chest	BUST
Cream of the crop	BEST
____ off (choke the chicken)	BEAT
Word with dead or wave	HEAT
	HEAD

	CRAP
Bottom-feeding fish	CARP
Give a fuck	CARE
Tortoise rival	HARE
____ and hearty	HALE
	HOLE

45 COMPOUND CUSSIN'

46 CONCEALED COCKS

In the year 672, a band of Nor**DIC K**nights on their way to rea**CH ODE**ssa were encamped at the snowy base of Mount Eze**KIEL. BASA**lt cliffs 1,000 feet high hemmed them in on three sides. Altof**OR, GAN**g leader of this paltry band, looked like any other Norse**MAN: HOOD**ed simply in stiff, drab leather. Ordinarily, he would **DON G**reen headgear and a trium**PHAL LUS**trous coat of armor—but not today. A passing shepherd would thin**K NO B**etter of it to see such a traveler in these parts and such anonymity would prove advantageous.

As day turned to night and Altofor stared deeply into the glu**M EMBER**s of his fading fire, he smiled to himself as he imagined ho**W ANG**ry the Odessans—who **PUT Z**ero thought into fortifying themselves from a southern attack—would be tomorrow morning and how much he'd en**JOY STICK**ing his blade through the chest of King **JOHN'S ON**ly living son, leaving hi**S NAKE**d, frozen corpse in the frozen slu**SH AFT**erward as a reminder to all that the **PEN IS** still not mightier than the sword.

47 HEATHER CHANDLER

Fuck me gently with a chainsaw.

47 DOROTHY PARKER

Tell him I was too fucking busy—or vice versa.

48 WORDOKU

E	A	G	C	D	H	B	U	O
C	U	D	B	O	E	G	A	H
H	O	B	G	U	A	E	D	C
O	B	H	A	C	G	D	E	U
G	E	C	D	H	U	A	O	B
U	D	A	O	E	B	H	C	G
A	H	O	U	B	D	C	G	E
B	G	U	E	A	C	O	H	D
D	C	E	H	G	O	U	B	A

49 DICKHEAD & HOLY SHIT

	DICK
Roll the ____	DICE
Word with wolf or straits	DIRE
Truth or ____	DARE
Got between the covers, say	READ
	HEAD

	HOLY
Word with pie or ass	HOLE
Word with garden or panty	HOSE
Party thrower	HOST
Word with money or body	SHOT
	SHIT

50 BASIC BITCH & FUCK SHIT

	BASIC
On a first-name ____	BASIS
Stereo knob	BASS
Big party	BASH
Word with bubble or bomb	BATH
Cookie quantity	BATCH
	BITCH

	FUCK
Pass the ____	BUCK
Do a street performance	BUSK
Slang for a woman's pubic hair	BUSH
Rear end	TUSH
____ the fuck up!	SHUT
	SHIT

---

51   OH NO! BETTE MIDLER!

A lot of people say that my life is wasted on me because I could be a bigger asshole than I am.

---

51   W.C. FIELDS

I don't drink water. Fish fuck in it.

---

52   TINA FEY

Photoshop is just like makeup. When it's done well, it looks great, and when it's overdone, you look like a crazy asshole.

---

52   ROBIN WILLIAMS

I wonder what chairs think about all day: "Oh here comes another asshole."

---

53   PRICK & LOSER

	PRICK
Haggler's concern	PRICE
California roll ingredient	RICE
____ and shine	RISE
Romantic flower	ROSE
Win, ____, or draw	LOSE
	LOSER

---

54   MILES DAVIS

Anybody can play. The note is only twenty percent. The attitude of the motherfucker who plays it is eighty percent.

---

54   ANONYMOUS

If you don't lie in bed at one in the morning and think "What the fuck am I doing with my life," you're doing something wrong.

---

55   CLOSE TO THE CHEST

---

56   ANONYMOUS

If you ever start thinking too highly of yourself, find your current position on Google Maps and zoom the fuck out.

---

56   DAN SAVAGE

Despite what Pope Benedict would have us believe, sex without love can be fucking amazing.

57 HERE, KITTY KITTY

58 TURKISH INSULT

Answer: PACKAGE

Quote: I'LL SHIT IN YOUR MOUTH!

60 SAY AGAIN?

61 STACEYANN CHIN

I'm a woman. That means I break hard. And mend like a motherfucker—all sexy and full of heartbreakingly beautiful scars.

61 DAVID BOWIE

I felt very puny as a human. I thought: "Fuck that. I want to be a superhuman."

62 GERMAN INSULT

Answer: BANANA

Quote: YOUR MOTHER SUCKLES PIGS!

64 QUEEN'S ENGLISH

65 FULL OF SHIT

66 BIBLICAL REBUS

holy shit

66 J.D. SALINGER

When you're not looking, somebody'll sneak up and write "Fuck you" right under your nose.

67 JOHN GREEN

I just did some calculations and I've been able to determine that you're full of shit.

67 CRANIAL PICTOGRAM

shit for brains

68 HARD WORD ARITHMETIC

0=U, 1=K, 2=F, 3=S, 4=H, 5=A, 6=E, 7=C, 8=O, 9=L

69 HARD WORD ARITHMETIC

0=S, 1=F, 2=R, 3=E, 4=M, 5=T, 6=Y, 7=A

70 WORDOKU

I	B	C	T	E	H	M	G	A
T	A	H	C	G	M	I	E	B
M	E	G	A	B	I	T	C	H
A	M	E	H	T	B	G	I	C
H	T	I	M	C	G	B	A	E
G	C	B	I	A	E	H	M	T
E	G	T	B	M	A	C	H	I
B	H	M	E	I	C	A	T	G
C	I	A	G	H	T	E	B	M

71 FOUR-LETTER WORDS

72 HARUKI MURAKAMI

Don't feel sorry for yourself. Only assholes do that.

72 STEPHEN KING

FEAR stands for fuck everything and run.

73 NOVEL TERMS

74 POETIC PROFANITY

75 TOUGH SHIT ...

	TOUGH
Look but don't ____	TOUCH
Cry of pain	OUCH
"Thank you very ____!"	MUCH
Iditarod command	MUSH
Buttocks	TUSH
Closed tightly	SHUT
	SHIT

76 PISS & BREATH

	PISS
Quarterback's throw	PASS
Glasgow girl	LASS
Flog with a whip	LASH
BDSM restraint, maybe	LEASH
Dissolve by percolation	LEACH
____ around (considerate act)	REACH
Whale's leap	BREACH
	BREATH

77 ARCHAIC ASSHOLES

78 CZECH INSULT

Answers:
BRAD PITT and PAUL RUDD

Quote: SMOKE MY COCK!

80 QUEBEC CUSSES

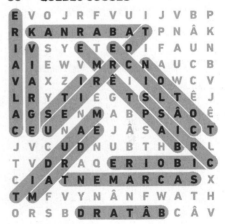

81 CLASSIC OATHS

82 GEORGE CARLIN

Life gets really simple once you cut out all the bullshit they teach you in school.

83 JIM C. HINES

Freedom of speech does not protect you from the consequences of saying stupid shit.

84 DIRTY-SOUNDING ANIMALS

```
  B       P           J
C O C K E R S P A N I E L         T
  O       A           C           I
  B       C           K           T
  Y       O       F A R T U L U M
    B     C       S               O
    U     K   T   S H I H T Z U
    G         U   O               S
  B E A V E R     C R A P P I E
    R         D   N
    A       P U S S Y C A T
    N         S   T
    U             O
    S P E R M W H A L E
                  D
```

86 BADONKADONK

87 WORDOKU

U	A	G	O	K	W	N	F	C
O	C	N	A	F	U	W	K	G
W	F	K	C	N	G	O	U	A
K	G	A	F	O	N	U	C	W
F	U	C	K	W	A	G	O	N
N	W	O	G	U	C	F	A	K
C	O	W	U	G	K	A	N	F
A	N	F	W	C	O	K	G	U
G	K	U	N	A	F	C	W	O

88 SHIZNIT

```
    D E E P S H I T
            I                   L
B     D     L           S       I
U     I     E A T S H I T       T
L     D     O                   T
L O A D O F S H I T             L
S     L     S         O         E
H O L Y S H I T         Y       S
I     S     I         S         H
T     S H I T S H O W           I
      I               I         T
S H I T L I S T
```

90 HIDDEN ASSES

```
    C     A     C A S S I D Y
    L     S             U
L A S S I E       N       T
    S     A       G       R     C
    S     S       L       E     A
F I R S T C L A S S             S
    F     I     O     S     P   S
    I     N     M A S S A G E
    E           P     E     S   T
    D     O N A S S I S         T
                S               E
P I C A S S O
```

92 ROBERT DOWNEY JR.

Listen, smile, agree, and then do whatever the fuck you were gonna do anyway.

93 BANKSY

Think outside the box, collapse the box, and take a fucking sharp knife to it.

94 WORDOKU

I	A	O	G	W	M	R	C	N
W	C	M	N	I	R	G	A	O
R	N	G	O	C	A	I	M	W
G	W	N	M	A	C	O	I	R
M	I	C	R	O	W	A	N	G
A	O	R	I	G	N	C	W	M
C	R	I	W	N	G	M	O	A
O	G	W	A	M	I	N	R	C
N	M	A	C	R	O	W	G	I

95 RAYLAN GIVENS

If you run into an asshole in the morning, you ran into an asshole. If you run into assholes all day, you're the asshole.

95 FREDDIE MERCURY

I'm just an old slag who gets up every morning, scratches his head, and wonders what he wants to fuck.

96 WORDOKU

E	P	C	G	F	U	R	I	K
R	I	F	E	P	K	U	G	C
U	G	K	R	C	I	F	P	E
K	F	G	P	E	R	I	C	U
P	U	R	I	K	C	E	F	G
I	C	E	U	G	F	K	R	P
F	K	P	C	I	E	G	U	R
C	E	U	F	R	G	P	K	I
G	R	I	K	U	P	C	E	F

97 LEWIS BLACK

Each of us is full of shit in our own special way. We are all shitty little snowflakes dancing in the universe.

97 MEL BROOKS

I've been accused of vulgarity. I say that's bullshit.

98 GERMAN INSULT

You are a chicken that got fucked in the ass!

99 TIM WIGGINS

Everybody carries around bags of shit. You can either leave those behind or stink for the rest of your life.

100 REFLECTIVE REBUS

ass backward

100 ANGELINA JOLIE

If being sane is thinking there's something wrong with being different, I'd rather be completely fucking mental.

101 CHINESE INSULT

Fuck your ancestors to the eighteenth generation!

102 DEB CALETTI

Your sibling, after all, is the only other person in the world who understands how fucked up your parents made you.

102 JONATHAN FRANZEN

The one thing nobody can take away from you is the freedom to fuck up your life whatever way you want to.

103 ERICA JONG

I'm just trying to lead my own fucking life if I can manage to find it in all this confusion.

104 DANIEL RADCLIFFE

I used to be self-conscious about my height, but then I thought, fuck that, I'm Harry Potter.

105 CHRIS ROCK

Religion in society is like salt. A little bit is good, but too much will fuck up your food.

105 PICTURESQUE PICTOGRAM

bullshit artist

106 LARS ULRICH

If you'd stop being a Metallica fan because I won't give you my music for free, then fuck you.

107 J.A. KONRATH

One of the greatest journeys in life is overcoming insecurity and learning to truly not give a shit.

107 JOHNNY DEPP

Just keep moving forward and don't give a shit about what anybody thinks. Do what you have to do—for you.

108 WORDOKU

O	B	E	N	S	A	H	K	D
A	S	N	H	D	K	O	E	B
D	H	K	E	O	B	S	N	A
B	E	A	S	N	D	K	O	H
H	D	S	K	A	O	N	B	E
K	N	O	B	H	E	A	D	S
E	O	B	A	K	S	D	H	N
N	A	D	O	E	H	B	S	K
S	K	H	D	B	N	E	A	O

109 WORDOKU

E	B	D	T	S	A	R	H	I
S	I	A	R	H	E	T	D	B
H	R	T	D	I	B	E	A	S
R	E	B	A	T	H	I	S	D
I	T	S	E	B	D	A	R	H
A	D	H	I	R	S	B	E	T
D	S	I	B	E	R	H	T	A
B	H	R	S	A	T	D	I	E
T	A	E	H	D	I	S	B	R

110 ERNEST CLINE

People who live in glass houses should shut the fuck up.

111 ANTHONY BOURDAIN

I want to keep the assholes in my life to an absolute minimum, if not zero. That's worth real, real money—to not have assholes in your life.

112 CONNER SMITH

You can spend your whole life looking down avoiding shit or you could just look up and not give a damn.

112 WIZ KHALIFA

I don't chase after anyone. If you wanna walk out of my life, then I'll hold the fucking door open for you.

113 ROBERT PLANT

All we knew about Elvis was that he sang like a motherfucker—and that was all that mattered.

114 ERNEST HEMINGWAY

I write one page of masterpiece to ninety-one pages of shit. I try to put the shit in the wastebasket.

115 GEORGE CARLIN

We buy shit we don't need with money we don't have to impress people we don't like.

115 PHILIP LARKIN

Poetry is nobody's business except the poet's—and everybody else can fuck off.

116 GREEK INSULT

Answer: WHIPPED

Quote: FART ON MY BALLS!

118 CHERYL STRAYED

The best thing you can possibly do with your life is to tackle the motherfucking shit out of it.

118 MERLIN MANN

The Internet's made of IP addresses, opinions, and assholes.

119 NEVILLE FLYNN

Enough is enough! I have had it with these motherfucking snakes on this motherfucking plane! Everybody strap in. I'm about to open some fucking windows.

120 RUDY FRANCISCO

It doesn't matter if the glass is half full or half empty—there's water in the cup. Drink that shit and stop complaining.

120 DAVID SEDARIS

If you're looking for sympathy, you'll find it between shit and syphilis in the dictionary.

121 CONOR McGREGOR

I simply speak the truth. I'm an Irish man. We don't give a fuck about feelings.

122 DYLAN MORAN

Never try the local thing. You know why it's local? Because it's shit—that's why it's local.

122 PITCHER PICTOGRAM

shit hitting the fan

123 DOWN-AND-OUT REBUS

shit out of luck

123 *THE WALKING DEAD'S* BUD

If you have to eat shit, best not to nibble. Bite, chew, swallow, repeat. It goes quicker.

124 GILLIAN FLYNN

I am not angry or sad or happy to see you. I could not give a shit. You don't even ripple.

124 A.S. KING

The world is full of assholes. What are you doing to make sure you're not one of them?

125 BULGARIAN INSULT

Get fucked by a horse!

126 OUR ORIGINS

What Darwin was too polite to say, my friends, is that we came to rule the earth not because we were the smartest or even the meanest but because we have always been the craziest, most murderous motherfuckers in the jungle.

STEPHENKING SWORDSWALLOWER WONDERWOMAN CATHERINEZETAJONES THEBEACHBOYS MUMMIFICATION HOWIMETYOURMOTHER WARRENBEATTY CHESTERCHEETAH THESAURUS TWEET TESTES VALUEMEAL STATUES EVERAFTER SAUTEED TUBES

128 @SHITMYDADSAYS

I like the dog. If he can't eat it or fuck it, he pisses on it. I can get behind that.

129 ED SHEERAN

If someone tells you to change yourself, tell them to go fuck themselves.

129 HENRY MILLER

When shit becomes valuable, the poor will be born without assholes.

130 AFRIKAANS INSULT

Suck on my hemorrhoids and wait for better days!

131 LARRY DAVID

You know who wears sunglasses inside? Blind people and assholes.

131 TROUBLE A-BREWIN' PICTOGRAM

shitstorm

132 AMHARIC INSULT

You are the fatty layer on my warm milk!

Rough translation: I have absolutely no use for you!

133 BRET EASTON ELLIS

All it comes down to is this: I feel like shit but look great.

134 LEWIS BLACK

In New York City, where I've lived far too long, fuck isn't even a word—it's a comma.

134 ALAN BENNETT

How do I define history? It's just one fucking thing after another.

135 HENRY ROLLINS

Half of life is fucking up. The other half is dealing with it.

136 CASUAL PICTOGRAM

shoot the shit

136 JIM THOMPSON

Life is a bucket of shit with a barbed-wire handle.

137 STEPHEN FRY

The short answer to that is "No." The long answer is "Fuck no."

138 TONI MORRISON

You wanna fly, you got to give up the shit that weighs you down.

139 JOAN CRAWFORD

Don't fuck with me, fellas. This ain't my first time at the rodeo.

140 GRANDMA'S GEM

Like my grandmother always said: "Your opinions are valid and important. Unless it's some stupid bullshit you're being shitty about, in which case you can just go fuck yourself."

JENNYLAWSON SUNDAYBLOODYSUNDAY ROCKYHORROR SHAWSHANK HOTTUBTIMEMACHINE RADIOACTIVITY EUCALYPTUS LIFEISBEAUTIFUL SUGGESTION MONDALE SUPERSTITIOUS PILGRIMS

142 GEORGE CARLIN

I don't have pet peeves—I have major psychotic fucking hatreds.

143 HUNTER S. THOMPSON

It's a strange world. Some people get rich and others eat shit and die.

144 DIRTY-SOUNDING PLACES

```
            H           C L I M A X
C O C K B U R N         O
            M       I   I
    D       P   I   N   S       S
    S H I T T E R T O N         P
    L       U   N   E   C       R
M I D D E L F A R T     O       E
    O       I   C       V       A
    C       P   M O R E H E A D
B U M P A S S   U       O       E
    M           R       O       A
    M           S       K       G
T I G H T S Q U E E Z E         L
    N           R               E
    G
```

146 FUNNY AS …

Shit is the tofu of cursing and can be molded to whichever condition the speaker desires. Hot as shit. Windy as shit. I myself was confounded as shit.

DAVIDSEDARIS FRIDAYTHETHIRTEENTH PROUDLYWEHAILED HIGHDEFINITION FASTFOODCHAINS KOWTOW BACCHUS MEMENTO STITCHES CONSENSUS SESSIONS

148 JONATHAN WINTERS

Life is a shit sandwich. But if you've got enough bread, you don't taste the shit.

149 ERNEST HEMINGWAY

The most essential gift for a good writer is a built-in, shockproof shit detector.

150 DAVID SEDARIS

When shit brings you down, just say "Fuck it"—and eat yourself some motherfucking candy.

151 ANONYMOUS

Don't call a woman a bitch. Call her an asshole. It still gets your point across and it's not sexist.

152 FIRST-WORLD PROBLEMS

We got so much food in America, we're allergic to food. Hungry people ain't allergic to shit. You think anyone in Rwanda's got a fucking lactose intolerance?!

CHRISROCK ANYWAYYOUWANTIT FEARANDLOATHING LEONARDODICAPRIO GEORGECARLIN CUCKOOSNEST OPTICALILLUSION ETOUFFEE GOTHAM GENTLEMEN GONEWITH

154 POLISH INSULT

Answer: ATLANTA

Quote: YOU FUCK HEDGEHOGS!

156 CHUCK WENDIG

Know your limits, then take those limits, wrap them around a hand grenade, and shove them up the ass of a velociraptor. Because, really, fuck limits.

WEIRDALYANKOVIC RICKYGERVAIS HIROSHIMA FASTANDTHEFURIOUS ADOLLARSHORT SOUTHDAKOTA WETHEPEOPLE ELEMENTS ATTACHMENT BUNSEN PUMMEL

158 ELIZABETH WURTZEL

I feel like … I came off the assembly line flat-out fucked and my parents should have taken me back for repairs before the warranty ran out.

LIMERICK NANTUCKET YESTERDAY FRANCISFORD LEWINSKY HOFFMAN ALASKA VERMONT ALABAMA

DEEPSOUTH EIFFEL RATHER BEEPER OUTOFTHEBLUE

160 FRENCH INSULT

Answer: HEMMED

Quote: I PISS ON YOUR BUTT CRACK!

162 LOOK AROUND

Before you diagnose yourself with depression or low self-esteem, first make sure that you are not, in fact, just surrounded by assholes.

WILLIAMGIBSON WHENHARRYMETSALLY RETURNOFTHEJEDI OKTOBERFEST SPOUSES ANACONDA ODYSSEUS FUTURE SUREFOOTED FOUREYES STORIES

164 KEEP IT PG

```
        S
B  HOLYHECK
U    U  R  J
L  S  C  I  U
L  O  K  M  D  J
S  N  SHITAKE
PHOOEY  N  S  E
I  F    Y  P  P
T  A  S    R  E
   G  U    I  R
  FUDGENUGGETS
   N  A    S
     FRACK    T
```

166 ALLITERATIVE ALLURE

```
GOOCHGOBLIN
     O
 FUCKFACE  H
     K     O
S DICKDIPPER
H    H     S
I  NADNIBBLER
T    F     H
S    E     U
TATERTITS  M
A          P
I  BUTTBATTER
N          R
```

167 FILTHY PHILIAS

Acrotomophilia: Amputees

Gerontophilia: The elderly

Chremastistophilia: Getting mugged

Dacryphilia: People crying

Eproctophilia: Flatulence

Formicophilia: Crawling insects

Hybristophilia: Criminals

Maschalagnia: Armpits

Narratophilia: Obscene words

Stigmatophilia: Body piercings/tattoos

Trichophilia: Hair

Urolagnia: Urination

168 ICELANDIC INSULT

Answer: DETECTIVE

Quote: HOP UP YOUR OWN ASS!

170 BOOB EUPHEMISMS

High Beams
Sweater Stretchers
Frost Detectors
Bobbsey Twins
Gerber Servers
Traffic Stoppers
Frontal Lobes
Jogging Partners
Congo Bongos
Siamese Twins
Shoulder Boulders
Meat Mountains
Thunder Jugs
Shirt Turnips
Milk Missiles
Jiggle Bags
Monkey Bumps
Double Bubbles
Boobic Mounds
Party Pendulums

172 DAN CARR

You're fine. It's in your capacity to have a messed-up life or not. Decide to be good, and everyone else can go fuck themselves. Don't let them get you.

LARRYTHECABLEGUY
YOUONLYLIVEONCE SKYDIVING
THEPHANTOMMENACE ONEPIECE
FOURFIFTEEN EGOTIST METOO
AREACODES DEVOTEDTO SUEDE STUDS

174 DUTCH INSULT

Answer: GWB

Quote: I FART IN YOUR DIRECTION!

176 ANTHONY LICCIONE

There are four kinds of people to avoid in the world: the assholes, the asswipes, the ass-kissers, and those that just will shit all over you.

THEWOLFOFWALLSTREET
SHUTTERISLAND THEDEPARTED
THEAVIATOR JOHNWILKES POLKA
VUITTON HORSESHOES PUSSY ALIASES
DISHES HOOSIERS

178 FINISH THAT QUOTE

You need a license to buy a dog or drive a car. Hell, you need a license to catch a fish. But they'll let any **butt-reaming asshole be a father**. — Tod Higgins, *Parenthood*

The only reason I did this is because you're my nephew and I love you. If it were anybody else, they would've gotten that intervention **through the back of their fucking head**. — Tony Soprano, *The Sopranos*

I bet you're the kind of guy that would fuck a person in the ass and not even have the goddamn common courtesy to **give him a reach-around**. — Gunnery Sgt. Hartman, *Full Metal Jacket*

Let me tell you something: There's no nobility in poverty. I've been a rich man and I've been a poor man. And I **choose rich every fucking time**. — Jordan Belfort, *The Wolf of Wall Street*

Now when you yell at me, it makes me nervous. And when I get nervous, I get scared. And when **motherfuckers get scared**, that's when motherfuckers accidentally get shot. — Jules Winnfield, *Pulp Fiction*

Wish in one hand and **shit in the other** one. See which one fills up first. — Willie T. Soke, *Bad Santa*

180 CHUCK PALAHNIUK

Nothing drives people crazier than seeing someone have a good fucking life.

180 BOB HUGHES

There's nothing more life-affirming than getting the shit kicked out of you.

181 CROATIAN INSULT

Go back inside your mother's pussy!

182 FRENCH CURSES

183 SEVEN-LETTER WORDS

184 YIDDISH INSULT

Answer: FLUFF

Quote: GO SHIT IN THE OCEAN!

186 FIVE-LETTER WORDS

187 EIGHT-LETTER WORDS

188 PENN JILLETTE

There's nothing better ... in the world than someone whose life was fucked up and you do a little something and now their life isn't.

188 GORDON RAMSAY

You've got every right to be slightly fucked off about it. Because I would be if I cooked that shit.

189 COURTNEY LOVE

If I fuckin' die without having written two, three, or four brilliant rock songs ... I don't know why I lived my life.

189 FRANK ZAPPA

People are basically shitty. It's when they prove it over and over again that it gets obnoxious.

190 ROMANIAN INSULT

I would dry my dirty underwear on your mother's crucifix!

191 SURROUNDED BY ASSHOLES

Galoshes
Abolishes
Shoelaces
Falsehoods
Hailstones
Lion's share
Close shave
Hot flashes
Shallowest
Kosher salt
Blasphemous

192 STEPHEN KING

Consider the Great Wall of China, if you will: one stone at a time, man. That's all. One stone at a time. But I've read you can see that motherfucker from space without a telescope.

192 HARLAN ELLISON

I still work on a manual typewriter, by choice, and to those who consider me a Luddite, I say: "Fuck you *and* yo mama."

193 AMY WINEHOUSE

It's not important to me to make other people at ease. I am difficult, but that's 'cause I don't really give a fuck.

193 MITCH HEDBERG

If you find yourself lost in the woods— fuck it, build a house.

194 SPANISH CURSES

195 SIX-LETTER WORDS

```
E S S B X Y P P A R C N W
O H P E T S U T A H S S A
C I O A Z S K A K H A P N
F T O V K B C T M R V Y K
U T G E G E U L G G F P E
C Y E R I C F F N F E R R
K Z V K H U F K I C R M E
E O O A X O W T K L E E S
R O S A G E S E H I T M S
D L L A I I R G F M O B I
K F J N E N N X M A O E P
E T E S T E S A S Y C R M
C R O T C H L A S S B A G
```

196 BILLY CORGAN

I don't necessarily believe that the sting of failure is a bad thing. It gives you a certain amount of freedom to just say fuck it!

196 TOM ROBBINS

I'll never write another novel on an electric typewriter. I'd rather use a sharp stick and a little pile of dog shit.

197 KEN KESEY

The job of the writer is to kiss no ass, no matter how big and holy and white and tempting and powerful.

197 GEORGE CARLIN

This country is full of nitwits and assholes. You ever notice that? Nitwits, assholes, fuckups, scumbags, jerkoffs, and dipshits. And they all vote.

INDEX

Because you've always wanted to see an index of how many times "fuck," "shit," and "ass" appear in a book.